COLLECTOR'S ENCYCLOPEDIA OF

English China

IDENTIFICATION & VALUES

COLLECTOR BOOKS
A Division of Schroeder Publishing Co., Inc.

MARY FRANK
GASTON

On the cover: from top, Pitcher, 6", Strawberry Lustre pattern, circa 1850, $150.00 – 175.00; pitcher, 5", Diamond Jubilee commemorative for Queen Victoria, circa 1892, $200.00 – 300.00; coffee can, circa 1795, $200.00 – 225.00; tea pot, enamel floral pattern, circa 1820, $425.00 – 475.00. At left: Coffee pot, 10", Chelsea grape pattern, circa 1845 – 1856, $150.00 – 175.00.

Other Books by Mary Frank Gaston

The current values in this book should be used only as a guide. They are not intended to set prices, which vary from one section of the country to another. Auction prices as well as dealer prices vary greatly and are affected by condition as well as demand. Neither the author nor the publisher assumes responsibility for any losses that might be incurred as a result of consulting this guide.

Searching For A Publisher?

We are always looking for people knowledgeable within their fields. If you feel that there is a real need for a book on your collectible subject and have a large comprehensive collection, contact Collector Books.

COLLECTOR BOOKS
P.O. Box 3009
Paducah, Kentucky 42002-3009

www.collectorbooks.com

Copyright © 2002 by Mary Frank Gaston

Contents

Dedication

To Jerry and Jeremy and Amber

Acknowledgments

A number of people provided photographs and information for this book on English china. I would like to express my thanks to those who have been so helpful.

A. & B. Auctions, Inc., of Marlboro, Massachusetts, sent catalogs and results from their auctions, which specialize in a variety of types of English china. Their catalogs provide excellent information and background on the pieces offered for sale. The company sent photographs as well, and I appreciate their cooperation.

Susan Bragg Antiques at the Antique Pavilion in Houston, Texas, graciously set aside time for me to visit and view her collection and select pieces which were photographed by my husband, Jerry. Susan specializes in Mason's Ironstone china, and I appreciate the knowledgeable information she furnished on examples from that firm.

Mr. and Mrs. John Keck, collectors of British Royalty Commemoratives, permitted us to photograph from their extensive collection and also provided detailed information about the various pieces and their history. I appreciate being able to have access to their collection.

McKinney Avenue Antique Market, Dallas, Texas, where I was allowed to spend two days photographing English china from the booths of their dealers, many of whom offered interesting examples of various kinds of English china.

Anne Pratt Slatin sent photographs of her Chelsea Grape collection which helped to add another dimension to this book. She also sent photographs of several other items of English china. I thank her not only for her photographs but also for advising me to contact two other collectors who became contributors as well.

Gwen Steapp, a very knowledgeable collector and dealer of Wedgwood, graciously took time to let us photograph from her collection. Her sales lists are very informative and reflect her research on each piece.

Sara Stickler and J.B. Queen, owners of DeWitt Hotel Antiques in Oak Hill, New York, generously sent photographs of a wide assortment of English china with informative notes about each piece. Their contribution was instrumental in spanning and bringing together the various components I wanted to include in this book. I appreciate their time and effort.

Mr. and Mrs. Robert Yerby who are collectors, not only of English china, but Limoges porcelain as well. I came into contact with Mr. Yerby while working on my third edition of *Limoges Porcelain.* I was very happy to learn of their English china interest. Many of the transfer pieces are from their collection. Mr. Yerby enjoys the study of marks and can be counted on to supply interesting examples and provide pertinent details for each.

Other contributors I would like to thank are these, listed in alphabetical order.

Brenda L. Bentley	Edna Koppenhaver	Barbara J. Singer
The Browns	James Lang	Harriet Stone
The Calubys	Roy T. Leitza	Gloria Swanson Antiques
Cindy Cherwront	Robin Mitchell	Stephanie L. Sytsema
Edith Clanton	Pete Pardoe	Gail Thurmon-Lansdown
Phil Cummins	Ernie Pauscher	Margaret Vanlier
Carmella Doughtery	Andrew J. Pye	Susan E. Wallace
Priscilla Gimple	Connie Reeder	Marcie Williams
Judy Grant	Linda Richard	Sarah M. Zafra
Sean J. Holland, III	Debbie and John Sherwood	
Dorothy P. Humphrey	Joyce Shillings	

I thank my publisher, Billy Schroeder, Collector Books, for publishing my twenty-first title. I thank Lisa Stroup and her staff for their work and assistance on all of my books. I thank my husband, Jerry, for once again photographing many of the examples featured here and as always, for his continued help and support.

Preface

I am very pleased to write this book about English china. My interest in English ceramics began over thirty years ago when I had the opportunity to live in England for almost a year. My husband, Jerry, was doing research for his doctoral thesis at various universities throughout England, and thus we had the opportunity to travel widely. Going to local antique markets and shops on the weekends fascinated us. We began to ship our "finds" home, not caring that the shipping charges far outweighed the prices we had paid or the intrinsic value of the pieces in most instances! Some years later, after I had started writing about Limoges porcelain and R.S. Prussia china, I had the opportunity to return to my interest in English china by writing books on Blue Willow and Flow Blue. While those two types of English china remain highly popular among American collectors, they represent only two collecting specialties out of an infinite number of collecting categories of English china.

In fact, it is rather daunting, or even arrogant, to say one is writing a book about English china. The subject is so broad and varied. When I wrote about Limoges porcelain, the subject was about a particular type of porcelain made in a particular city in France. Similarly, the majority of English potteries are confined to one area of England, the Staffordshire district. Although only hard paste porcelain was made in Limoges, many different ceramic bodies were made in Staffordshire. While Limoges porcelain was generally decorated by hand painted or transfer techniques, English china used not only those methods, but many others as well.

English China is one of, if not the most, general and open-ended designation of any china collecting specialization. The term has various meanings for individual collectors. In fact, because of its broad nature, collectors rarely refer to themselves as collectors of "English china." There are too many manufacturers, too many patterns, and too many methods and types of decoration. Rather, collectors concentrate on a specific facet of English ceramics which is personally appealing. For example, Tea Leaf patterned ironstone, Gaudy ironstone, the Blue Willow pattern, Flow Blue china, Historical Views, and Royal Commemoratives are just a few kinds of English china which are collected because of a specific type of technique or decoration. Basalt wares and parian are examples of English china collected because of their body type. Royal Worcester, Spode, and Wedgwood are only three among hundreds of factories whose wares are collected because they bear marks of those factories.

It is evident that numerous subjects are covered by the term, English china. There are specific reference books devoted not only to different manufacturers but also to many specific collecting categories. Additionally, many of the subjects have national and international collector groups and newsletters. The sheer breadth and depth of English china make it really a fascinating subject. It is apparent from the displays of china offered for sale that interest in all types of English china is increasing. Moreover, many collectors are becoming more eclectic in their acquisitions. While one may have begun collecting Flow Blue china, for example, an interest in a particular Flow Blue Oriental pattern may have spawned an interest in other English Oriental designs in other colors. Likewise, a collector of Royal Commemoratives may become interested in English stonewares or loving cups.

For this book, I have focused on the decoration of English china. The examples represent not only a number of different types and methods of decoration, but also span several eras of production, various body types, numerous manufacturers, different objects, and a wide range of values.

The first chapter discusses general and basic information regarding the English china industry which is pertinent to collectors. Types of ceramic bodies, decorating techniques, and marking methods are included. A glossary style list of terms, with brief definitions, relating to those three areas is at the end of Chapter 1.

The second and third chapters are devoted to general and specific decorations. Molded Designs and Relief Decorations compose Chapter 2 and include several collecting categories such as White Ironstone, Chelsea Grape china, Majolica, and Cameo décor. Enamels, lustres, and gilded examples are found in Chapter 3. Overglaze polychrome enamel decoration, "Gaudy" wares, and copper, pink, and strawberry lustres are included.

In Chapter 4, the emphasis is on Oriental decorative themes and patterns. This chapter is divided into two major sections. Polychrome Oriental designs form the first part with an emphasis on Mason's patterns. The second part covers monochrome Oriental designs which were not only made in blue, but also in other colors such as black and mulberry. Chapter 5 focuses on decorative themes and patterns that are non-Oriental designs. These are arranged by decorative themes such as animal, figural, scenic, floral, and fruit. The polychrome Oriental designs include both transfer and non-transfer patterns. The monochrome Oriental designs and other non-Oriental patterns are primarily underglaze transfer patterns.

English china novelties are the subject of Chapter 6. Figural china such as Toby jugs and Staffordshire animals and figures come under this category.

Chapter 7 is devoted to a special collecting category, Royal Commemoratives. This specialty was included because it well exhibits an area which reflects the English china industry. Examples can be found in a variety of body types, from simple pottery to bone china. Pieces exhibit a variety of decoration types and techniques, such as molded, relief, and *pâte sur pâte*. Colorful glazes, lustres, gilding, and both monochrome and polychrome transfer designs are found on the commemoratives. The subject matter, the specific sovereign, usually identifies the time period when the item was made, even if the example is unmarked. The objects themselves are of interest. Whiskey bottles as well as loving cups, urns, and pitchers are just a few of the ceramic items made by English potters to commemorate the weddings, coronations, jubilees, and deaths of British royalty.

An index to manufacturers follows the Bibliography. By consulting this index, collectors will get an idea of the various types of decorations used by many of the factories. An Index to Various Types of Decoration is also included as well as an Index to Pattern names.

The time periods for examples in this book basically range from the late eighteenth century through the early twentieth century. Manufacturer's marks are shown with many of the examples. A large number of pieces were unmarked, especially those dating from the late 1700s; circa dates are noted for most of these. Information and dates of the marks shown, or referred to, are based on the definitive work of Geoffrey A. Godden's *Encyclopedia of British Ceramic Marks on Pottery and Porcelain*, 1964. Collectors are referred to his book for information on various companies represented here.

Please note that this book is not designed to be a comprehensive study of the collecting categories or manufacturers represented. But this general survey of English china will illustrate the wide scope of the production of the English china industry. The basis for the influence of that industry on the American market, and hence, American collectors, becomes apparent. Hopefully, this book will whet the appetites of both seasoned and new collectors to the almost limitless possibilities for increasing or forming an interesting personal collection of English china.

Mary Frank Gaston
P.O. Box 342
Bryan, Texas 77806

Chapter One
Collecting English China

Ceramics have been made in England for thousands of years. Burton (1975, p. 10) notes that very simple pottery produced over an open flame was made in England as early as 3500BC and that the same method was used for another three thousand years. For most American collectors, however, the English china industry refers to the Staffordshire district which is composed of small towns which have been engaged in making china since the mid-1600s. From primitive beginnings, the English china industry developed and prospered. The availability both of clays, suitable for making china, and coal, which was needed to fire the ovens, were the underlying reasons why the English china industry became concentrated in the Staffordshire area. The discovery of the underglaze transfer printing process and accessible routes of transportation for shipping finished products are major reasons why that industry thrived. By the early 1800s, England was the chief source of ceramic table wares for Americans.

By the mid-1800s, Americans had turned to china made in other European countries, such as France and Germany. Although an American china industry also developed during that period, Americans continued to demand imported china, and Japan began to take over a large part of the American market after 1891. Thus while England did not enjoy a monopoly of the American china market, English china did not cease to be imported. Consequently, English ceramics are well represented in today's American collectible china market. England remains a world leader in manufacturing china, and although many of the historic companies have gone out of business or been consolidated with larger firms, the concentration of factories still resides in the small towns, such as Stoke, Burslem, and Hanley in Staffordshire. The Staffordshire area is a major tourist attraction. One can board a bus and travel to many of the factories and museums in the area where exhibitions and the china making process of earlier days, as well as currently, can be viewed.

There are three major elements important to consider when collecting English china. Those are ceramic body types; decoration; and manufacturers and their marks. These three elements are, of course, interrelated, and one element may take precedence over another, depending on the particular area of specialization. Some collections are composed of a certain body type, such as ironstone or parian. Other collections may be based on the assorted or specific type of production of a particular manufacturer, such as any china made by Josiah Wedgwood, or only Wedgwood's jasper ware. But the type of decoration to the body of the china is probably the most important factor for a collector. The decoration on a ceramic body is often the first point of recognition which immediately identifies a piece of china as an example of one's particular interest. The decoration speaks before the body type or maker's mark may be determined. Collectors instantly recognize Cameo décor, Daubed Ware, Copper Lustre, Majolica, Gaudy Welsh, Mulberry china, Flow Blue china, the Indian Tree pattern, and so forth, depending on the particular interest of the collector. A closer examination of these three elements, body type, decoration, and manufacturer's marks, provides some general and basic information for collectors.

Ceramic Body Types

English china was manufactured in all three body types common to the china industry. These include earthenwares, stonewares, and porcelain, both soft paste and hard paste. To understand the differences among these ceramic body types, a brief discussion of each is necessary.

Earthenwares are made from many different types of natural clays, including kaolin, ball clay, and Cornish stone. Earthenware is fired at temperatures below 1200 degrees Centigrade. If a glaze is applied, the object is re-fired at a temperature below 1100 degrees Centigrade. Earthenware is opaque, that is, you cannot see through it. Technically, earthenware is a type of pottery which has a porosity of more than five percent.

Earthenwares may be waterproof if they are covered with a glaze. The glaze, however, is separate from the clay body. The glaze and body are not fused together completely during the glaze firing. Consequently, earthenwares are the weakest of the three ceramic body types. Majolica is an example of glazed earthenware. A clay flower pot is an example of unglazed earthenware.

Stoneware is made from natural clays which are of a sedimentary type and are fined grained and quite plastic. Stoneware differs from simple earthenware in that it has a porosity of less than five percent because stoneware is fired at extremely high temperatures ranging from 1200 to 1400 degrees Centigrade. A glaze is applied to the earthenware body before the first firing, and during that first firing, the body and the glaze fuse together and become vitrified, that is, like glass. Additional glazes can be added to stoneware bodies after the first firing, but they are not necessary because the vitreous quality is achieved during the first firing. Stoneware, like earthenware, is opaque, but stoneware is heavier than earthenware. Stoneware is also harder and more durable. Basalt, ironstone, and certain types of crockery are examples of stoneware.

Porcelain, the third type of ceramic body, is actually considered to be a special type of stoneware. That is because porcelain is also fired to a state of vitrification. Stoneware is not fired to a state of translucency as porcelain is, however. Porcelain objects are first fired at temperatures around 900 degrees Centigrade. After this first firing, the object is translucent, but it is not vitreous. The translucent quality is obtained from the type of ingredients used in making the body paste. After the first firing, the resulting product is called bisque or biscuit, meaning unglazed. Figurines are examples of porcelain which are often found with bisque or unglazed bodies. To attain vitreosity, the object must be baked a second time with a glaze and re-fired at temperatures of 1300 to 1500 degrees Centigrade. Porcelain differs from the other two body types, earthenware and stoneware, in that it is translucent, and that is the reason why it has become common to differentiate china into three body types. Porcelain is also lighter in weight than stoneware and stronger or more durable than earthenware.

Porcelain, moreover, is divided into three types: *bone paste, soft paste,* and *hard paste.* The paste type depends on the type and percentage of basic ingredients used as well as the manufacturing process. All three types are translucent in both the bisque and glazed states. They are light in weight, but are still strong. They are also vitreous, if glazed.

Bone paste (or bone china) was so called because its principal ingredient was made of an ash made from calcined animal bones. This bone ash constitutes at least fifty percent of the paste with such materials as china clay and feldspar making up the rest of the formula. Bone paste is stronger than soft paste porcelain, and the manufacturing process is also less expensive. The product is first fired, unglazed, to a translucent state at a temperature of over 1200 degrees Centigrade. It is fired a second time with the glaze at a lower temperature, below 1100 degrees Centigrade. The Spode, Worcester, and Wedgwood factories introduced bone china in England during the latter part of the 1700s and early 1800s. England is still the center for this type of production although manufacturing processes have been modernized.

Soft paste refers to the degree of temperature needed for the firing process which is lower than the temperatures required for firing bone paste and hard paste porcelain. Soft paste porcelain is not actually "soft." Objects are first fired at about 1100 degrees Centigrade. After the glaze is applied, the object is re-fired at a lower temperature. Due to the lower firing temperatures, this type of porcelain is not as durable as bone paste or hard paste. English factories such as Bow and Chelsea made soft paste porcelain during the 1700s.

Hard paste porcelain was considered to be a natural porcelain because its ingredients exist in the earth. That was not the case with bone china which used ash from animal bones in the paste or the early soft paste mixtures which used glass in the paste. Kaolin, a type of earth containing hydrated aluminum silicates, accounts for 50 percent of the hard paste mixture. Feldspar is the other important natural ingredient. Feldspar comes from a rock, and it is necessary not only for the body paste but also for the body glaze. Feldspar adds strength to the paste, allowing the object to be fired at a high temperature and to become translucent. The glaze contains a larger percentage of feldspar than the body paste. It also contains quartz which is necessary for the glaze and paste to melt together and fuse into one entity. The object is then vitreous or like glass. Hard paste objects are first fired at around 900 degrees Centigrade. The second firing with the glaze is at temperatures of from 1400 to 1600 degrees Centigrade. Most European hard paste porcelain, historically, has been produced in Germany, France, and Austria. Although a few English factories, such as Bristol, made hard paste porcelain, English china is primarily found with earthenware, stoneware, or bone china bodies.

A list of the major ceramic body types found in English china are briefly defined here as well as some other terms associated with ceramic bodies.

English Ceramic Bodies, Types, and Terms

Basalt, a black, unglazed stoneware with a matte finish, of Egyptian origin, but Josiah Wedgwood gained renown for this type of ware in English ceramics during the latter part of the eighteenth century.

Biscuit, items made of clay, earthenwares or porcelains, which have been fired only once and are unglazed.

Bisque, unglazed china, a term usually applied to hard paste porcelain.

Bone china, a translucent china incorporating bone ash in the paste. Bone china is the principal type of china made in England.

Ceramic, items composed of clay and fired at high temperatures.

China, popularly refers to any kind of ceramic body, but the word actually is meant only for hard paste porcelain.

Crazing, a network of lines visible on the surface of a glazed earthenware body caused by the clay body and glaze not being fused together completely during the firing process.

Cream Ware or Queen's Ware, an earthenware body, covered with a clear tin glaze, which was quite durable and a light yellow or "cream" in color. Josiah Wedgwood introduced this ware circa 1760. He named it "Queen's Ware," for Queen Charlotte after receiving her patronage in 1765.

Crockery, utilitarian pottery generally made of earthenware.

Earthenware, technically means one of the two classes of pottery, and which has a porosity of more than five percent. Earthenwares are composed of various types of natural clays and fired at high temperatures. They are opaque and not vitreous, although they may be glazed. Because earthenwares are not vitreous even when glazed, the surface can be penetrated. This accounts for the "crazing" or network of lines often visible on earthenware bodies.

Fired, to bake formed clay items at high temperatures.

Hard paste, a translucent type of porcelain made of kaolin and feldspar, which is vitreous if glazed.

Ironstone, a type of stoneware incorporating ground iron slag with the clay mixture resulting in a hard body with a shiny finish which was opaque and very durable. Ironstone was patented in England by the Mason Company in 1813. Other companies made similar wares but used different names to describe them, such as granite ware and stone china.

Jasper Ware, a type of unglazed white stoneware containing barium sulphate, introduced by Josiah Wedgwood circa 1774. Wedgwood discovered that colors could be added to the paste, resulting in colored bodies. Later the white stoneware was dipped in color rather than having the color incorporated into the clay mixture.

Majolica, an earthenware with a special glaze containing tin. The body is brown in color but is decorated with monochrome or polychrome glazes. Molded and relief work on the body are also typical. Mintons is responsible for introducing this type of ware in England about 1850, but Majolica's origins are several hundred years earlier, beginning in Italy, and called *faience*.

Mold or mould, a form made in a desired shape to hold the clay paste and thus give form to the clay object.

Opaque, meaning that light does not pass through the object, the opposite of translucent.

Paneled, refers to ceramic bodies which are molded with definite angular sides rather than being totally round in shape.

Parian, an unglazed hard paste porcelain made to imitate marble. The body was well adapted to sculpturing busts, figures, and other decorative objects. Several English factories made this type of body from the mid-1800s, after it was introduced by Copeland, in 1846 (Boger, p. 256).

Paste, the basic clay mixture of any china before the clay is shaped and formed.

Porcelain, technically a form of stoneware because it is fired to a vitreous state. Porcelain is distinguished from stoneware, however, because porcelain is translucent. The term porcelain is used to designate true or hard paste porcelain whose principal ingredient is kaolin, a type of clay containing hydrated aluminum silicates. Little true porcelain was made in England.

Pottery, objects formed from clay and fired at high temperatures. The two major categories of pottery are earthenwares and stonewares.

Redware, a red clay earthenware.

Semi-porcelain, china with a glazed body, but not translucent and not totally vitreous.

Semi-vitreous, not completely vitreous, ware that is not waterproof and not like glass.

Soft paste, a type of porcelain fired at lower temperatures than hard paste porcelain.

Spur or stilt marks, small protrusions usually found in three places on either the back or front of a piece of china which was caused by the clay supports which were used to separate objects in the kiln during the firing process.

Stone china, properly refers to the stoneware body introduced by Spode, circa 1805, which had a brilliant glazed surface, was opaque, hard, heavy, and durable. The term "stone china," however, evolved as a name used by other English manufacturers for china similar to Spode's or to Mason's ironstone china.

Stoneware or stone ware, technically the second major classification of pottery. Stonewares have a porosity of less than 5 percent because feldspar and quartz are added to the clay mixture causing the body to become vitrified when fired at a high temperature during the first firing. Stonewares are not fired to a state of translucency, however, and thus are opaque.

Terra cotta, red clay earthenware which is not glazed, like a flower pot.

Vitreous, impervious to liquids, like glass. Stonewares and porcelains are completely vitreous because the glaze and the body are fired together until they fuse to form one entity. Thus the outer glaze cannot be penetrated.

Decorations

Decoration on English china is usually divided into non-transfer decoration and transfer decoration. Although a large percentage of English china represents transfer decoration, non-transfer decoration was used on many types of collectible English china. Such decoration encompasses a variety of methods and is by no means limited to hand painted themes, which are the obvious opposite of transfer decoration. In fact, non-transfer decoration can be roughly divided into two kinds, unpainted and painted. Unpainted decoration relates totally to the body of the china where some form of decoration is made directly on the china body or applied to the body before it is fired. Very simple to quite complicated decoration can be achieved by different methods. Examples include molded relief or intaglio designs, machine turned or incised work, and the application of other materials or separate molded decoration affixed to the body of the china. Flowers and leaves created separately in a realistic image and applied to a vase or a pitcher are examples of applied décor. Applied decoration can also refer to something added to the entire body of an object, such as salt added during the glaze firing to create a special effect of a pitted surface on the ceramic body. Unpainted decoration enhances the surface of the china, which in turn can be further decorated by painting or other methods. For non-transfer decorations, the application of color is by hand. The color can take various forms such as enamel and gilt and can be applied either before or after an object is fired or before or after an object is glazed, depending on the type of decoration desired. Colored enamel glazes, resist-applied lustres, and handpainted decorative themes are some examples of this form of non-transfer decoration. Handpainted work ranges from simple lines and sponged-on color, to floral designs, to full portraits or scenes.

Transfer ware may be considered synonymous with English china because so much china was historically decorated by that method, and transfer wares do make up a very large part of the American collectible English china market. The "Willow" pattern is probably the best known example of a transfer pattern. Transfer decoration is also called lithography. In lithography, a design is etched on a stone or copper plate. The design is then filled in with ink, and a thin piece of paper is pressed onto the design. The paper with the imprint of the design is then "transferred" to a piece of pottery. Any of the three types of ceramic bodies can be decorated with a transfer pattern.

The transfer method of decoration has been in use in England from about 1750. In the beginning, transfers were first applied over the glaze of the china body and then touched up or entirely painted. The overglaze transfers could become worn off, however, and were not totally satisfactory as a form of decoration. It was not until about 1760 that the underglaze transfer printing process was successful. Underglaze handpainted decoration had been used in China for hundreds of years. The Chinese had discovered that the color blue, derived from the mineral cobalt, was the one color which could withstand the high degrees of heat necessary to fire the glaze and still maintain clarity of the design under the glaze. That is why Oriental porcelains were decorated with blue. The English, wanting to emulate the Chinese style, designs, and colors, also found it was necessary to use the color blue for underglaze decoration. The underglaze decoration was permanent, and the process revolutionized the china decorating industry in England. It not only made decoration easier and less expensive, but it allowed for a number of items to be decorated with the same design. By the mid 1800s, other underglaze colors, such as black, brown, and mulberry, were perfected. Later, multicolored underglaze transfers were possible.

Terms relating to the china decoration process which are used in this book and frequently found in relation to English ceramics are briefly defined.

Decorating Methods and Types

Applied, any decoration which is formed separately and then affixed to a ceramic body.

Bas-relief, low relief work where the decoration does not stand out too much from the body of the china.

Basket-weave, a ceramic body decoration where the clay has either been woven by hand or molded with a pattern to resemble a woven basket.

Bat printing, a transfer technique of decorating china used during the late 1700s. A "bat" of glue picked up the engraved design from the copper plate and then the "bat" with the design was transferred to a ceramic body. This particular type of transfer is characterized by a stippled design which is then dusted with a colored powder. The object is then fired to melt the colored powder and to set the decoration.

Brush stroke, a term used to refer to some handpainted decoration, typically associated with handpainted Flow Blue patterns.

Chinoiserie, decorations with an Oriental motif.

Cobalt blue, a color used to decorate ceramics which was derived from an oxide of the mineral cobalt. The substance is brown in color when it is applied to the ceramic body, but the high heat during the firing process transforms the color to a deep blue.

Combed, a handpainted decorating technique of drawing or pulling color over a ceramic body to produce a mottled or marbled effect, used from the 1600s.

Daubed, a handpainted decorating technique of daubing color randomly on a ceramic body.

Dipped, a term used to refer to coating a ceramic body with a colored glaze.

Enamel, colors composed of glass and various minerals used to decorate ceramics. The glass gives a vitreous quality and shiny look while the color depends on the particular mineral used in the glass mixture. Colored enamels may be applied to a glazed or unglazed ceramic body. The object must then be re-fired to set the color.

Flow Blue, a decorating technique used chiefly on underglaze blue transfer ware. This method originated in Staffordshire from the late 1820s. By adding certain chemicals such as saltpetre, borax, and white lead to the kiln during the glaze firing, the cobalt blue color used for the underglaze pattern would "run," obscuring the detailed lines of the design, resulting in a smudged, flowing effect.

Gilding, to decorate with gold.

Glazes, the liquid, glassy substance applied to ceramics to make them impervious to liquids, and also used in various colors to decorate ceramics.

Gaudy, basically a term referring to brightly colored polychrome decorations found on earthenware or stoneware bodies.

Handpainted, refers to colored decoration applied by hand to china. Handpainted decoration can be either over or under the glaze. Early transfer designs were filled in or accented with handpainted work.

India red, a burnt-orange color.

Jackfield, a red earthenware with a black glaze.

Japonaise, decoration emulating the Japanese style.

Intaglio, a molded body design which is concave rather than convex.

Lustres or lusters, a metallic finish on ceramic bodies achieved by applying a coating, or design, composed of a particular metal or mineral, such as copper, which is reduced during the firing process until only the metal remains as the decoration. Lustres are found in a variety of colors including gold, pink, purple, and silver, depending on the substance used.

Machine turned, designs on ceramics formed by machine rather than by hand.

Marbled, mottled glazes on ceramics made by "combing" the color over the body surface.

Mat or matte, a glaze or finish which has a dull finish.

Monochrome, decoration on china composed of just one color on the ceramic body which can actually refer to a colored glaze over all of the body or a pattern or design in just one color over the white body; the Blue Willow pattern is a monochrome blue on white decoration.

Mulberry, a dark brown to dark purple color used for English underglaze transfer patterns from the 1830s to 1850s.

Openwork, body decoration where the clay is shaped to have a pierced rather than solid design, usually found around the border of an object.

Overglaze, any decoration applied on top of the glazed ceramic body.

Pâte sur pâte, paste on paste, an applied relief form body decoration made by applying layers of liquid slip until the desired shape is obtained. This form of decoration originated in France, but in England, Minton became known for this technique after the company hired a former Sèvres artist, Solon, circa 1870.

Polychrome, more than one solid color used to decorate china. The term can refer to either handpainted or transfer decoration.

Relief, ceramic body decoration where the clay body has decoration molded or shaped to stand out from the body in a raised or convex manner.

Reticulated, openwork, or perforated, ceramic body decoration.

Resist, refers to a decorating method whereby parts of a design are prevented from receiving color and remain undecorated, such as silver and lustre resist wares.

Salt glaze, an early type of glaze used on English stonewares which has a pitted surface caused by putting salt in the kiln during the firing process.

Sepia, a reddish-brown color used on early transfer patterns.

Slip, a liquid form of clay made with water and used as an early form of decoration on china. The liquid clay was applied by a quill to form designs.

Spattered, decoration made by dusting color on a ceramic body.

Sponged, color decoration applied by using a sponge to daub the color on the body surface.

Sprigged, a term used to describe applied relief decoration, where the decoration is formed separately from the body, then applied to the body and attached using liquid slip.

Stick, a handpainted decoration of lines painted or combed over the body surface.

Tapestry, a form of applied body decoration where a cloth is fired onto the body of the china resulting in a body having the same texture as the cloth. Although the cloth is destroyed during the firing, the imprint of its texture is left.

Transfer printing, indicates that designs or patterns have been engraved on copper plates, the grooves of the designs filled with ink or paint, after which the copper plate is heated and a soapy tissue paper is pressed into the engraved design, taken off, and in turn pressed upside down on an object which has been heated and coated with varnish and then heated so that the pattern will stick. After the object has dried, the paper is washed off, but the design remains — thus the design has been "transferred" from the copper plate to the object. Transfers on ceramics can be applied over or under the glaze.

Transfer wares, any china decorated with a transfer print, commonly refers to English printed china made during the eighteenth and nineteenth centuries.

Underglaze, decoration applied either by hand painting or transfer to the clay body before the glaze firing. Underglaze decoration is permanent.

Marks

Marks on English china are important for collectors so that not only the particular manufacturer can be determined but also the approximate age of the china. While a large percentage of English china is found with marks, collectors should be aware that many examples are found without marks, especially pieces made prior to 1800. Godden, 1964, notes (Plate Three) that printed marks on English china were not routinely used until after the mid-eighteenth century. Marks on English china were made in several different ways. They were either incised, impressed, handpainted, or printed. The first two methods incorporated the mark into the body of the china before it was fired. Handpainted marks and printed marks, made from transfers or stamps, were applied before or after the glaze firing of the china. If the marks were applied under the glaze, then the mark became permanent.

Because of Geoffrey Godden's extensive research regarding English ceramic marks, collectors of English china are easily able to identify and date most English marks with the assistance of his books, particularly the *Encyclopedia of British Pottery and Porcelain Marks*, 1964. Many of the English factories maintained precise marking systems which included not only the name of the pottery, but the month and year of production, the inventory or design number, and often an artist's mark. Tables are available to interpret such marks for companies like Minton, Royal Crown Derby, Wedgwood, and Worcester, to name a few.

Knowledge of several general facts about English marks is also useful, and a number of these are listed below. A few misconceptions, however, are common regarding English marks. One concerns English registry marks which have been used since 1842. An impressed or printed diamond symbol with letters and numbers, or just printed numbers prefaced with the initials "RD," are sometimes found on English china. These marks indicate that the pattern or mold of the object was registered with the British Patent Office in order to keep that particular pattern or mold from being copied by some other manufacturer. Godden (1964, pgs. 526 – 528) has printed tables for decoding the marks and numbers which can identify specific years. General books on marks also usually contain these tables. The registry marks are often misinterpreted, mistakenly thought to mean that if a piece has such a mark, that the particular piece was made in that particular year which corresponds to the registry number. The numbers only refer to when the design or shape was first patented. The same design or shape could have been used during many subsequent years, maintaining the original registry mark. Designs or shapes might also have been used prior to their registration. Also, not all china made from 1842 bears a registry mark. The registry marks are useful primarily as a clue only to the period when the pattern or shape was first invented.

Another error regarding English ceramic marks may be caused by marks which include a printed year. The designation of a year with a mark usually only indicates the year when the factory was first founded, often many, even hundreds, of years prior to when the piece bearing the year mark was made. The factory may have changed ownership several times and may not even have the original name. It was a common practice of ceramic factories, not only in England but in other European countries, especially during the late nineteenth and early twentieth centuries, to incorporate founding dates with their later marks.

The name "Wedgwood" can be misinterpreted when found as a mark on English china. Several companies used this name in their marks. The most famous Wedgwood company is the Josiah Wedgwood firm which was founded in 1759. His marks are not spelled with an "e" (Wedgewood) nor do they include the initial "J." or "& Co." William Smith marked china with "Wedgewood" (with an "e") after 1848 until 1855 (Godden, 1964, p. 583). Godden (1964, p. 687) states that a John Wedge Wood operated a pottery from 1841 to 1860 and used a mark that incorporated the name "J. Wedgwood." "Wedgwood" was also used by Podmore, Walker & Co. who eventually changed the company name to Wedgwood & Co. circa 1860. Enoch Wedgwood was the Wedgwood associated with that company, and thus the basis for that company's use of the name, see Godden, 1964, pgs. 501, 655. Collectors should realize, however, that Wedgwood marked china made by these other companies is still collectible. Examples, however, should not be attributed to the Josiah Wedgwood company.

Last, marks on modern reproductions present another point of confusion for collectors. Historically, ceramic marks have been copied, and often such examples are collectible today based on the age alone of the pieces. Today the collectible china market is heavily stocked with a large assortment of new china designed and often marked to replicate the old. Some of the current reproductions of English china include Majolica, Staffordshire figures, "flow blue," and the Blue Willow pattern as well as other scenic or "romantic" transfer designs. Some of the china with "misleading" English marks has been around for almost twenty years. It is understandable how new collectors might not be aware of or alert to those reproductions. Some of the china is not marked, but other examples often include a coat of arms mark printed with "Victoria" and "Ironstone Staffordshire England." This china has been made since the late 1960s by Blakeney Pottery Limited which is located in Stoke-on-Trent. Another mark used by the firm is composed of a large floral cartouche and includes the word "Romantic" and "Flo Blue, T.M. Staffordshire, England." The company specialized in Victorian reproductions. Mustache cups, shaving mugs, footbaths, bowl and pitcher sets, and cheese keepers are just a few of the items they produce.

There are a few general rules of thumb to remember regarding modern reproductions. Always be wary of any illegible mark. Some genuine marks, especially on flow blue china, are smudged, but today some marks are deliberately blurred. "Flo Blue" was never printed on china decorated with that special technique. Authentic Staffordshire figures are generally unmarked. Large offerings of the same pattern of similar Victorian type objects at flea markets and other antique outlets usually are a good indication that the china is new. Prices can also reflect new china. If the prices are low, such as twenty-five dollars for a cheese keeper, unquestionably the piece is new. Unfortunately, though, prices which genuinely old items would fetch are found on many new examples. When paying large prices for any collectible or antique item, always demand a money-back guarantee in the event the item may later be found to be a reproduction.

English Ceramic Marks, Types, and Terms

"England" is found in some English marks from the last quarter of the nineteenth century, but was used on all exported wares after 1891 to comply with American tariff laws.

Garter marks are printed marks, round or oval in shape, used by some English factories during the latter half of the nineteenth century.

Impressed marks are made in the form of initials or symbols and pressed into the ceramic body before it is fired.

Incised marks are cut into the ceramic body before it is fired.

Limited (Ltd.) is a word or abbreviation found in many English marks after 1880.

"Made In England" is noted by most authorities to definitely be of twentieth century origin. "Made in" and the particular country name are noted by the Kovels (p. 231) to have been required by English law on imported wares from 1887. But no specific requirement is noted for china exported from England or for china imported by the United States. Therefore "Made in" as part of a mark on English china does not specifically date from any one year. Thus some examples from the same historical period may have this mark and others will not.

Overglaze describes marks placed on an object after it has been glazed. Overglaze marks are handpainted or printed. Marks applied overglaze can be worn off or taken off.

Pattern names printed with marks were not used before the early 1800s.

Printed marks refer to marks made in the form of a transfer or stamp. Such marks can be applied either over or under the glaze.

Raised marks are those formed in relief on the body of the china before it is fired or formed separately and then affixed to the ceramic body before it is fired.

Registry marks are marks or numbers impressed or printed on English ceramics after 1842. Diamond-shaped marks were the first type used and were continued until 1883. After that time, the consecutive numbering system, prefaced with the initials "RD," was used. Tables to decipher such marks are found in general marks books. These registration numbers were assigned to companies in order to protect a shape or pattern design for three years, but the registry marks could continue to be placed on the china after that three-year period. When interpreted, these registry letters or numbers will identify the year such designs were first registered. Thus, the registry marks only indicate when the company registered the design, and it is possible that the design was used before it was registered. Many designs were never registered.

"Royal" is a word used in English marks after 1850.

Royal Arms marks are printed marks of coats of arms and were not used before the 1800s.

Staffordshire knot or bow knot refers to a bow-knot shape used to mark English ceramics during the 1880s.

"Trade Mark" is a term used in English marks primarily after the last quarter of the nineteenth century.

Underglaze refers to marks applied to ceramic bodies before they are glazed. Such marks are permanent and cannot be worn or taken off although they can be covered over.

Chapter Two

 # Molded and Applied Decorations

While this book is about the varied decorations found on English china, the first group of pictures may seem at odds with this subject, because they are of china void of any color. But studied closely, it is apparent that while the china has no color, it is, nonetheless, decorated. Imagine a fully decorated piece of china in terms of layers. Peel off those layers, starting with the outermost decorative element. The last layer would be a piece of blank china or white ware, referred to as "green" ware or "biscuit" because it is just the baked clay mixture. To preserve the body of the china, a glaze must be applied to this green ware. Or for stonewares, the glaze is actually part of the basic clay mixture, and the first baking results in a glaze covering. Although the glaze is protective, it is also decorative.

In English ceramics, one area of collector specialization is White Ironstone. The lustrous white glaze is the basic form of decoration. Examples have no type of colored enhancement. White Ironstone, however, may have molded or applied decoration, often referred to as embossed or relief work. Designs are usually simple and formed as part of the original mold, like the Davenport "Fig" platter. Food molds are particularly interesting and collectible on their own, in addition to being representative of White Ironstone. Their molded decoration is also basically simple in design.

More elaborate relief work can be seen in the Mason's Hunt Jug where both molded and applied decoration compose a detailed scene. Other types of English china are found absent of color. Salt glazed wares are one example. Salt was added to the glaze resulting in a small-pebbled body surface. Color can be added, of course, but salt glazed china is found in the white ware form as illustrated by the William Brownfield syrup jug. Creamware and other earthenware bodies can be found absent of color but with molded or applied decoration. The English potters, however, do not seem to have made and exported "blanks" to be purchased and decorated by American china painters during the late Victorian era as did other European china factories. The reason for this is because hard paste porcelain was the preferred body type, rather than the earthenwares, stonewares, and bone china made by the English manufacturers.

Following the unpainted white wares are other examples of molded and applied decorations. These pieces may exhibit, in fact, several different types and methods of decoration. Colored glazes, enamel finishes, and metallic lustres highlight or accent the molded or applied body decorations. Some random types as well as some specific collecting categories, such as Chelsea Grape and Majolica, are featured to portray a selection of molded and applied decoration. Another form of applied decoration, called Tapestry, was used by some English factories. A piece of textured fabric was fired onto the body of a piece of china, hence the name, tapestry. Such china bodies provide a unique background for other applied or painted decoration.

Probably the most recognized form of applied decoration is cameo ware. China decorated with classical figures, using this method, was made famous by the Josiah Wedgwood company. Basically, figures were formed in clay and attached to a china body. Wedgwood Jasper Ware identifies this particular collecting category. Jasper Ware is a type of basalt or stoneware with a shiny, grainy appearance. Other factories also decorated with applied figures, cameos, or flowers in that manner, and pieces are collected under the term of Cameo Ware. *Pâte sure pâte* is another form of applied decoration formed in a different manner by layering liquid slip on a china body to achieve a low relief decoration.

Molded and Applied Decoration on Unpainted Ceramic Bodies

W.H. Grindley coat of arms mark on soap dish, after 1891.

Plate 1. Soap dish with cover, White Ironstone, W.H. Grindley & Co., coat of arms mark, after 1891. **$20.00 – 25.00.**

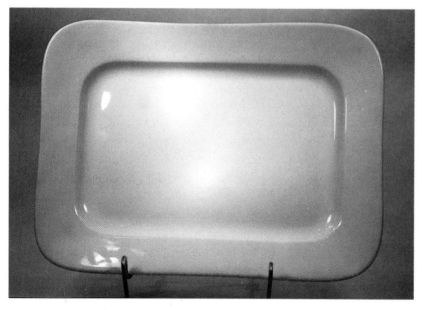

Maddock & Co. Royal Stone China mark on platter, circa 1906.

Plate 2. Platter, 15"l, White Ironstone, rectangular shape, Maddock & Co. **$70.00 – 90.00.**

Johnson Bros. mark on pitcher, circa 1891 – 1900.

Plate 3. Pitcher, 12"h, White Ironstone, scalloped neck with a wide paneled molded body design; a small flower applied between top and stem of handle, Johnson Bros. **$150.00 – 175.00.**

Jacob Furnival mark on platter, coat of arms with initials, circa 1845.

Plate 4. Platter, 16"l, White Ironstone, oval shape, marked by deep impression in the mold around the outer border, Jacob Furnival. **$70.00 – 90.00.**

Davenport impressed mark on octagonal platter, the numbers "5" and "6" are either side of the anchor, indicating a date of 1856.

Plate 5. Platter, 18"l, White Ironstone, octagonal shape, "Fig" pattern, molded fruit and leaf design spaced around outer border, Davenport. **$225.00 – 250.00.**

Plate 6. Pitcher, 5"h, White Ironstone, molded leaves and berries, unmarked, circa early 1900s. **$70.00 – 80.00.**

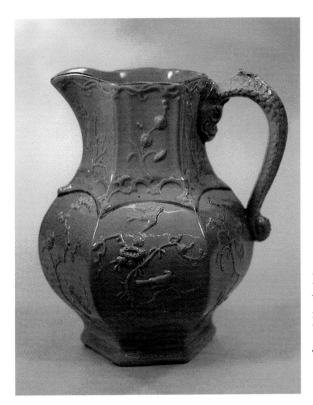

Mason's mark on jug, circa 1845.

Plate 7. Jug, 7½"h, flowers, vines, and birds molded in light relief decorate the ironstone body, Mason's. **$450.00 – 550.00.**

Plate 8. Jug, 7"h, ironstone china, heavy relief work depicting hunting dogs and intricate scenic designs around top, Charles James Mason. **$1,200.00 – 1,400.00.**

Charles James Mason mark on hunt jug, circa 1845 – 1848, with an applied pad mark impressed with "TOHO," a command for a hunting dog to "stop."

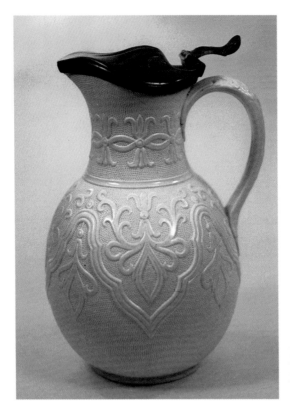

William Brownfield impressed mark on salt glazed jug with a diamond-shaped registry mark and cypher for the year 1862. "Tyrol" is also part of the factory mark, perhaps denoting shape or body design.

Plate 9. Syrup jug, 7"h, salt glazed stoneware, hinged metal lid, embossed scrolled work over body, William Brownfield. **$300.00 – 400.00.**

Plate 10. Mould, 7¼"l, Asparagus molded design, unmarked, circa early to mid-1800s. **$100.00 – 125.00.**

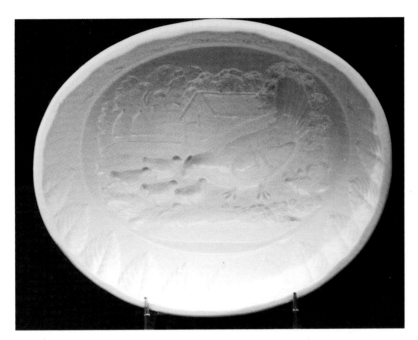

Plate 11. Mould, 7½"l, 3⅜"h, Hen & Chicks pattern, impressed "WEDGWOOD" mark, circa early 19th century. **$140.00 – 165.00.**

Plate 12. Plate, 9"d, cream ware, reticulated border with a molded basket-weave pattern, Wedgwood impressed mark with a year cypher for 1861. **$175.00 – 200.00.**

Molded and Applied Decoration Enhanced with Color

Plate 13. Creamer and Mug, earthenwares, simple beaded decoration on the creamer and machine turn work on the lower body of the mug forming a circular design. Two painted brown bands add a touch of color to the creamer. The dark brown glaze around the top of the mug was applied in a manner to leave an undecorated chain of geometric shapes to form a simple decoration, unmarked, circa 1820. Creamer, **$100.00 – 120.00 (mc)**; Mug, **$120.00 – 135.00.**

Plate 14. Pitcher, 6¾"h, salt glazed stoneware, unmarked, but attributed to Doulton's Lambeth factory, circa last quarter of the 19th century. The relief decoration features a child with a hat, a child on a horse, a leafy tree, and a windmill. The top third of the piece has a rust-brown glaze contrasting with the lighter buff color of the lower body and interior. **$100.00 – 125.00.**

Plate 15. Pitcher, molded leaf designs, enameled in green and a light tan form the pattern, separated by bands composed of small flowers painted in blue and white. A dark brown mottled glaze serves as the background. "Doulton, Lambeth, 1879" is impressed on the base, accompanied by the incised initials of the artist, "G.R.H." **$300.00 – 400.00.**

Plate 16. Mug, 4"h, decorated with colored enamels over applied figures and midsection. Pink lustre borders accent piece, unmarked, circa 1840. **$140.00 – 165.00.**

Plate 17. Pitcher, 6"h, relief design of a ram and sheep decorate body with raised berries at the top of handle and near the spout. A dark cobalt blue painted floral design overlaid with copper lustre is around the base and neck. The handle is formed like a twisted vine, unmarked, circa mid 1800s. **$225.00 – 250.00.**

Doulton & Slater's patent mark on pitcher, ca. 1886 – 1914.

Plate 18. Pitcher, 8"h, metal hinged lid; a tapestry finish, painted brown with gold accents, covers the body. White enameled flowers and green leaves form a pattern over the tapestry work. The impressed marks are "Doulton & Slater's Patent," and "Doulton Lambeth England," with the artist's initials "F.g." incised in script form. **$150.00 – 175.00.**

Plate 19. Pitcher, 11"h, brown tapestry finish. Applied flowers in blue and white leaves accent body and handle, marked with the same Doulton marks as on preceding example. **$225.00 – 275.00.**

View of applied decoration on handle of pitcher.

Chelsea Grape and Floral Patterns

Grapes and flowers in relief were a popular form of decoration on dinner ware made by several Staffordshire potteries from the 1830s. The floral and fruit designs were distinguished by a lavender blue finish. Often that color was accented or covered with a copper lustre as well. The blue color with, or without, the copper lustre against the very sharp white glaze on the ironstone body of the china makes a very striking decoration. The china was not made in Chelsea, and it is not clear just why that name became associated with this type of decoration. Most of the pieces are unmarked. Examples with figures as well as fruit and flowers can also be found. Several versions of the grape pattern were made. Prices are still quite affordable. Collectors may also refer to this type of decorated china as "Grandmother's Ware."

Plate 20. Coffee pot, 10"h, Chelsea Grape pattern with copper lustre, unmarked, but matches marked sugar bowl in following photograph. **$150.00 – 175.00.**

Plate 21. Sugar bowl, 8"h, matching coffee pot, marked with Edward Walley's printed coat of arms mark, see Godden Mark 3988, circa 1845 – 1856. **$125.00 – 150.00.**

Plate 22. Cup and saucer, Chelsea Grape with copper lustre, unmarked, circa 1830. **$25.00 – 30.00.**

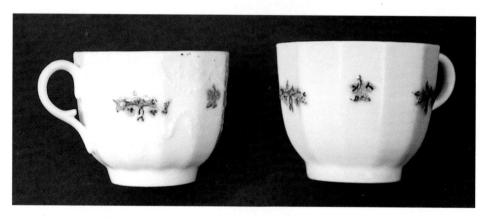

Plate 23. Cups, unmarked. **$15.00 – 20.00 each.**

Plate 24. Salad plates: left, Vase of Flowers motif with copper lustre; right, Chelsea Grape with copper lustre, unmarked, circa 1830s. **$20.00 – 25.00 each.**

Plate 25. Cake plate, 10" sq., another type of Chelsea Grape pattern with copper lustre. The handles are outlined by lightly embossed work, unmarked. **$25.00 – 30.00.**

Plate 26. Cake plate, 10"d, Chelsea Grape pattern, molded ribbed designs frame well and handles are outlined by rings, unmarked. **$25.00 – 30.00.**

Plate 27. Plates: left, 6"d; right, 8"d; unmarked, Chelsea Grape pattern. Note the embossed beaded garland design around the outer border of these plates. **Left, $12.00 – 15.00; right, $22.00 – 25.00.**

Plate 28. Tea pot, 8½"h, cup and saucer, and cake plate, 9"d, Chelsea Sprig pattern, unmarked, circa 1830. Tea pot, **$125.00 – 150.00;** cup and saucer, **$30.00 – 35.00;** cake plate, **$25.00 – 30.00.**

Plate 29. Plate, 6"d, and saucer, Chelsea Thistle pattern, unmarked, circa 1830. Left, **$6.00 – 8.00.**

Plate 30. Cup and saucer in the Thistle pattern, unmarked. **$30.00 – 35.00.**

Plate 31. Cake plate, 8¾"d, Thistle pattern, lightly embossed scroll work outlines handles on each side, circa mid-1800s, unmarked. **$25.00 – 30.00.**

Plate 32. Plate, 6¾"d, Chelsea type figural designs, impressed mark for T. Edwards, circa mid-1800s. **$10.00 – 15.00.**

Plate 33. Pitchers: left, 5½"h, Bird & Banner pattern, G. Phillips' mark, circa 1834 – 1848, **$60.00 – 70.00;** right, 5½"h, different Chelsea motifs including an urn with fruit, unmarked, **$35.00 – 40.00.**

Majolica

The term "majolica" refers to a special type of glaze applied to pottery which contains tin or lead. That type of glaze dates back about eight hundred years, first used by potters in Spain. The wares were exported from the port of Majorca, and hence the development of the name "majolica." A number of Staffordshire factories made majolica during the nineteenth century. Minton, Wedgwood, and George Jones are a few of the names associated with this type of production. But many examples were unmarked. The height of popularity for English majolica was during the mid Victorian era, although it was made in lesser quantity through the mid-twentieth century. Naturalistic shapes and classical designs with vibrant colors characterized English majolica.

Majolica represents another form of molded and applied decoration. The unique tin glaze imparts a mirror-like sheen to the bold colors which decorate the china. Early majolica glazes in England were opaque and applied to painted bodies. Later, colored majolica glazes were developed. Most of the decoration is polychrome rather than monochrome. Handpainted decoration could be applied over the glazed body. Wear may be evident on such examples. Values have increased over the last several years. Reproductions are also prevalent.

Minton impressed marks on jug.

Plate 34. Jug, 10"h, a deep yellow-gold monochrome finish covers this Minton jug. A figural and scenic theme in relief depicts a boy in an apple tree in a garden setting. Leaves and vines encircle the handle. The year, "1881," is impressed on the top border, evidently commemorating some event. The marks on the jug, however, are ambiguous. Theoretically, the marks should include 3 cyphers identifying the month, year, and potter. The marks on this piece, however, do not correlate with the Minton tables, see Godden Number 2699. **$450.00 – 550.00.**

Minton printed globe mark and registry mark for December, 1875 (A=December; S=1875) on Bamboo & Fan majolica plate.

Plate 35. Plate, 9"d, black reticulated outer border with a yellow basket-weave designed inner border. A white fan and green bamboo leaves decorate center on a black ground, and small birds and flowers accent the fan. The Minton pattern name, "Bamboo & Fan," is printed under the Minton globe mark. $150.00 – 175.00.

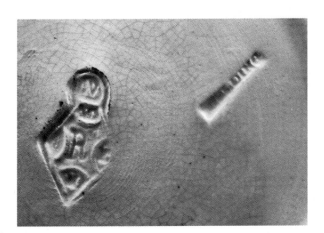

Impressed Registry Mark for plate at right.

Plate 36. Plate, 7½"d, two sculptured fans, a yellow butterfly, and small flowers decorate the pebbled surface. The impressed factory mark is illegible, but the registry mark indicates a date of 1882. $125.00 – 150.00.

Plate 37. Compote, 2½"h, 10"d (pedestal is not visible), embossed flowers and leaves surround a fan. The cobalt blue paint on the fan shows signs of wear, unmarked. **$300.00 – 350.00 (mc).**

Plate 38. Plate, 9½"d, decorated with beaded body designs and a floral motif in blue, greens, and mauve, "DAVENPORT" printed mark, circa mid 1800s. **$250.00 – 300.00.**

Plate 39. Leaf-shaped plate, heavily veined, polychromed in brown, yellow, and green, unmarked, circa early 1900s. **$150.00 – 175.00.**

Impressed monogram mark of George Jones on compote, circa 1861 – 1873.

Plate 40. Compote, 5"h, 9"d, a white finish surrounds the points of the large green leaf in the center of the dish. A yellow border trims the piece. These three colors are repeated on the stem and base in an irregular manner, George Jones. **$1,000.00 – 1,200.00.**

Plate 41. Basket, 8"h, 9"w, heavily ribbed body is decorated with a wide cobalt blue border highlighting small pink and blue flowers with green leaves in relief, unmarked, circa 1870. **$700.00 – 800.00.**

Plate 42. Bread plate, 12½"l, green leaves and small pink flowers decorate inner border on a bright yellow ground. The center of the plate and the outer border have a dark brown finish, unmarked, circa 1870. **$550.00 – 650.00.**

Plate 43. Plate, 12"d, molded figural scene of a man with a mug and a keg of beer. A light yellow glaze covers the center design with the outer border composed of shells covered with a dark brown glaze, unmarked. **$200.00 – 250.00.**

Pâte sur Pâte and Cameo Ware

Pâte sur pâte and cameo are two terms which refer to relief decoration. The differences between *pâte sur pâte* and cameo ware lie basically in the methods used to apply the decoration and resulting appearance on the decorations. *Pâte sur pâte*, the French term meaning "paste on paste," describes a form of *bas-relief* fashioned by layering white slip on a colored ceramic body. A low relief design is then carved from the layers. When the object is fired, the carved slip decoration emerges with a glassy or vitreous appearance in white against a colored body. The Minton Company became famous for this type of decoration in England during the last quarter of the nineteenth century when the firm hired a former Sèvres employee, Solon, to implement that French technique. Other English factories also decorated in that manner. Some used the technique even earlier than Minton, see Plates 44 and 48.

Cameo Ware refers to carved relief decoration which has been molded separately and then affixed to a china body. The cameos or relief decorations are made of the same material as the body of the piece, but the relief work is left uncolored or with a natural white finish. This relief work can be affixed, however, to a body which has a colored finish. The firing of the ware results in a piece of china which has relief decoration in white, but the finish of that decoration is the same as the body of the china. That is, while the *pâte sur pâte* emerges from the kiln with a shiny finish, the cameo affixed relief decoration comes out of the kiln with a matte finish like the body. Both forms of decoration are usually, but not always, found on stoneware bodies, variously called basalt, parian, or jasper ware. These types of china bodies are unglazed stonewares and have a hard grained surface.

Cameo Ware, in fact, is practically synonymous with Wedgwood's Jasper Ware although some other factories decorated in that style. Josiah Wedgwood invented the Jasper Ware body in 1874. His factory became famous for that form of stoneware decorated with relief decoration of classical figures which were molded and affixed or carved in a cameo manner. The white decoration on the colored bodies was quite striking. Dark blue and light blue bodies were most popular, but later other colors were used for the bodies. Historically, the colored finish of the stoneware bodies was achieved by firing with colored glazes which permeated the body. If broken, the break would show that the color was uniform through the body and not just on the exterior. Later, colored glazes were applied by dipping the china into a colored glaze. Consequently, such examples were white on the interior with a colored exterior.

Several examples of Wedgwood's cameo decoration on Jasper Ware are shown here. These represent china made during the eighteenth and nineteenth centuries. No marks are shown for the Wedgwood pieces, but approximate dates are noted. A piece of early Cream Ware from an unknown manufacturer, an early Alcock parian pitcher, a late Adam & Co. parian pitcher, and a Robinson & Leadbeater rose bowl illustrate other examples of cameo and *pâte sur pâte* relief decoration.

Plate 44. Mug, Cream Ware, *pâte sur pâte* classical figures in a pastoral setting are framed with a simple silver lustre floral design, unmarked, circa late 18th century. **$150.00 – 175.00.**

Plate 45. Rose bowl, 2¾"h, 3⅝"w, the applied leaf and acorn decoration stands out in high relief from the dark green glaze overlaid on the parian body. The mark on the piece is "R & L, Stoke on Trent," attributed to Robinson & Leadbeater prior to 1891. **$150.00 – 200.00.**

Samuel Alcock & Co. mark on pitcher with the title of the decoration and an English registry mark for April 27, 1847.

Plate 46. Pitcher, sculptured figural decoration, "Naomi and her Daughters-in-law," on a parian body overlaid on a lavender-blue ground, Samuel Alcock & Co. **$3,000.00 – 3,500.00.**

Copeland mark on pitcher with a registry number for 1899.

Plate 47. Pitcher, 6"h, golfing motif in *pâte sur pâte*. The mocha-colored parian body is overlaid with a dark green glaze which accentuates the relief figures, Copeland. **$325.00 – 375.00.**

Davenport printed mark on cup and saucer, prior to 1830, see Godden Mark 1191.

Plate 48. Cup and saucer, *pâte sur pâte* decoration of a cherub and an "interlocking circles" border pattern on a lavender ground with gilded trim, Davenport. **$275.00 – 300.00.**

Plate 49. Ink stand with ink pots (missing lids), classical figures, the "Three Graces" and various Cupid scenes form relief decoration on the cobalt blue dipped body, Wedgwood, circa 1760 – 1780. **$1,000.00 – 1,200.00.**

Plate 50. Ewer, 9"h, classical figures on a cobalt blue dipped body, Wedgwood, circa 1840. $900.00 – 1,000.00.

Plate 51. Candle sticks, 7"h, figures of Apollo with lyre and Urania with globe and staff on a cobalt blue dipped ground, circa 1840 – 1870, Wedgwood. $550.00 – 600.00 set.

Plate 52. Biscuit barrel, 5½"h, classical figures applied over a light blue dipped ground, Wedgwood, circa 1840. $350.00 – 400.00.

Plate 53. Cache pot, 5 ¼"h, cameos of George Washington, Benjamin Franklin, and Thomas Jefferson decorate three sides on a cobalt blue dipped ground, Wedgwood, circa 1876. **$350.00 – 400.00.**

Plate 54. Ferner, classical figures, Aesculapius and student, on a light blue dipped ground, Wedgwood, circa 1890. **$350.00 – 400.00.**

Plate 55. Vase, 5"h, famous Portland shape, cobalt blue dipped body, rare white, twisted rope handles, circa 1850 – 1870. **$600.00 – 700.00.**

Plate 56. Match box, 4⅜"l, with striker inside lid, classical figure on a cobalt blue dipped ground, Wedgwood, circa 1790 – 1820. **$250.00 – 300.00.**

Chapter Three

Enamel, Gilt, and Lustre Decorations

The types of decoration presented in the preceding chapter focused on incorporating the decoration into the body of a piece of china, either by molding the designs into the clay before the piece was fired or by applying and attaching separately formed decoration which protruded from the ceramic body. This chapter looks at color decoration applied to the clay body after it has been fired. Applied decoration of this nature is what we usually consider to be decoration, because it consists of colors on the china body in the form of either glazes, certain designs, or patterns. In the previous chapter, the molded or relief work was the dominant decorative feature, even if the china was also decorated with colored enamels and glazes. While the bodies of the following examples might also have some molded design or applied work, the colored glaze, design, or pattern is the primary focal point of the piece.

The earliest types of painted decoration were applied after the clay body had been fired and consisted of simple designs and patterns. A variety of terms define some of these early decorating techniques. Consequently, these terms identify specific collecting categories of English china today. The descriptive words refer not only to the look of the decoration but also to the method of how the colored decoration was applied. Brush stroke, combed, daubed, dipped, feathered, stick, marbled, and sponged identify a number of these early decorating techniques. These decorations were made of colored slip, which was actually a liquid clay composed of ingredients like the body but diluted to form a thin paint-like consistency. While this early type of decoration of English pottery was inexpensive and much of it aimed at the American market, today collectors value such pieces for their age and primitive appearance. Examples of several are included in the first group of photographs with a brief definition of each.

Enameled decoration refers to vitreous paints which are composed of glass and various metals which result in different colors. The enamels are applied to a china body which has already been fired. The enamels can be applied either over a glazed or an unglazed body. After the enamel decoration has been applied, the piece is re-fired at a very low temperature. Enameled china ranges from full body glazes to simple floral and fruit designs, which were totally hand painted, to more elaborate decorations which were often outlined by a transfer design and then filled in with the colored enamel. Enamel decorations span the color spectrum from pastels to brilliant shades. Usually the enamel patterns consist of several colors and are referred to as being polychromed decoration. Sprig patterns, cottage décor, and gaudy wares are a few of the collecting categories of overglaze enamel decoration selected for this chapter.

Some other overglaze decoration consists solely of gilded work, that is the application of gold leaf as a trim or pattern. Gold leaf was ground into a powder and mixed with honey which resulted in a thin paint which could be applied to a china body. The piece was then re-fired at a low temperature. After firing, the color of the gold was dull, so the gold was polished or burnished to give a shiny appearance. Gilding also was added to all types of other decoration, and it is apparent that gilt work became the most widely used form or trim for all types of decorated china.

Lustre decoration refers to the metallic qualities of a glaze which result in a shiny or iridescent look. Metal oxides were used for this purpose. Platinum was the base metal required to obtain a silver lustre, and gold was the metal used for copper and gold lustres. Pink lustres were made by adding Purple of Cassius to gold. The Tea Leaf patterns are a type of English lustre decoration which are probably the most popular among American collectors. A simple leaf design was painted with a copper lustre on white ironstone bodies. Lustres, however, could cover the whole body or merely form a simple border or trim. Some patterns on lustre wares were achieved by "resist," techniques where sugar is mixed with the paint. When the piece is fired to set the glaze, the sugar dissolves and prevents the lustre from covering the pattern, hence, it "resists" the lustre. Thus, the lustre outlines or surrounds a design or pattern.

The Chelsea Grape patterns are another form of lustre decoration. The relief work on those pieces caused them to be placed in the preceding chapter, but it could very well be argued that those examples could be here because the lavender-blue lustre is a primary component of the decoration. Moreover, as shown in the examples, copper lustre was often added as well. Strawberry Lustre patterns, representing the pink lustres, compose yet another category of lustre decoration.

The majority of china shown in this chapter was made during the late eighteenth or early nineteenth century. Most of these are unmarked, and thus only a few marks are shown, and those represent the latter part of the period. Prices vary with some being quite nominal while others may realize hundreds of dollars.

Simple Decorating Techniques

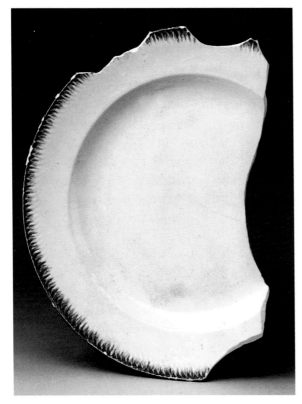

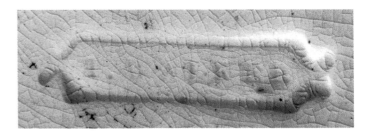

Impressed mark of Thomas Walker on plate.

Plate 57. Plate, 10"d, earthenware, cobalt blue has been brushed on the edges of this piece in what is called a "Feather" or "Feather Edge" pattern. This type of pattern was made by brushing or "combing" the color around the edge of the china. This piece has the impressed mark of Thomas Walker, circa 1845 – 1853. The broken example is shown to illustrate the pattern and decorating technique. If in good condition, **$60.00 – 75.00.**

Plate 58. Covered cache pot, 1¾"h, dark green and yellow-orange colors are "daubed" on randomly over the entire surface. This particular design is called the "Egg & Spinach" pattern, unmarked, circa 1760. **$275.00 – 300.00.**

Plate 59. Plate, 8¼"d, dark brown and yellow paints have been "combed" together to produce a "marbled" decoration on both sides of the plate, unmarked, circa 18th century. **$200.00 – 300.00.**

Reverse side of marbled plate.

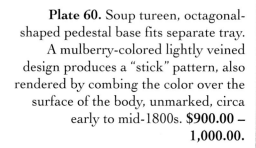

Plate 60. Soup tureen, octagonal-shaped pedestal base fits separate tray. A mulberry-colored lightly veined design produces a "stick" pattern, also rendered by combing the color over the surface of the body, unmarked, circa early to mid-1800s. **$900.00 – 1,000.00.**

Plate 61. Plate, 9½"d, an example of "brush stroke" or handpainted floral pattern in cobalt blue which "flows." Copper lustre has also been used to outline veins on the leaves, unmarked, circa mid-1800s. **$140.00 – 160.00.**

Plate 62. Tea pot, unmarked, circa 1830. This piece had a transfer decoration on the body, but the example is pictured here to show the "spatter" or "sponge" decorating technique which is visible on the spout, lid, and handle. **$400.00 – 450.00.**

Enameled and Gilded Decoration

Plate 63. Syrup pitcher, 6"h, Britannia metal lid, a black glaze covers the body with narrow bands of gilt accenting the middle, base, and handle of piece, unmarked. This particular decoration is called "Jackfield," or "Redware," terms applied to a glossy black glaze covering a "Redware" (terra cotta) body which was popular from the mid-eighteenth century. **$200.00 – 250.00.**

Plate 64. Coffee cans, porcelain, made by the Worcester factory, circa 1790. Three different gilded decorations are shown. **$150.00 – 175.00 each.**

Plate 65. Ice cup, porcelain, decorated with green enamel and gilt, unmarked, attributed to Worcester, Flight Barr & Barr period, circa 1813 – 1840. **$175.00 – 200.00.**

Plate 66. Master salt, 1¾"h, footed, unmarked, circa 1770, enameled flowers, in bright colors, accented with gilded trim. **$300.00 – 350.00.**

Plate 67. Dessert plate from a set of 12, attributed to Davenport, circa 1840, representing a botanical theme in enamels and gilt. **$1,800.00 – 2000.00 for the set.**

Plate 68. Sauce boat, 5"l, porcelain, attributed to New Hall Porcelain Works, circa 1800, enamel and gilt were used in this "cottage" style decoration. (That type of decoration, however, does not always incorporate a house or cottage, rather the term refers to a simple form of hand-painted decoration). **$200.00 – 225.00.**

Plate 69. Cup and saucer, porcelain, unmarked, attributed to the Worcester factory, circa 1830, multicolored enameled flowers and gilt designs. **$350.00 – 425.00.**

Plate 70. Hydra (water) jug, 4¼"h, unmarked, attributed to Mason, circa 1820. White enameled flowers in relief and gilt decorate the dark blue glaze which is known as Mason's "Mazarine Blue." **$425.00 – 475.00.**

Plate 71. Vase, 7¾"h, unmarked, attributed to Mason, circa 1840, Mazarine Blue glaze and gilt décor. **$500.00 – 600.00.**

Sprig Patterns

Simple handpainted flowers or "sprigs" were painted in polychrome enamels over the glaze. These designs are usually found on porcelain or soft paste bodies. Many Staffordshire potteries decorated in this manner. Most examples, however, are unmarked. The work is considered to be from the early 1800s.

Plate 72. Tea pot, 9"h, earthenware, attributed to Scottish Potteries, circa 1780. Small floral sprig designs are on a ribbed body, yellow-gold borders outlined in black. **$375.00 – 400.00.**

Plate 73. Dish, porcelain, attributed to the New Hall Porcelain Works, circa 1810. The multicolored floral sprigs in the center of the dish are complemented by a border pattern composed of a sprig garland and half pinwheel design in similar colors. **$100.00 – 120.00.**

Plate 74. Dish, porcelain, attributed to New Hall, circa 1810. A chain of dark green leaves forms an inner border for the sprig pattern. **$100.00 – 125.00.**

Plate 75. Plates, 6"d, soft paste, "ADAMS" impressed mark, circa 1785 – 1805, see Godden Mark 18. A dark green and magenta sprigged floral pattern decorates center and outer border. **$20.00 – 25.00 each.**

Plate 76. Cup and saucer, soft paste, unmarked, circa early 1800s. The cup has a similar magenta and green design as the preceding plates while the leaves on the saucer are larger. **$25.00 – 30.00.**

Plate 77. Sugar bowl, 5"h, soft paste, unmarked, magenta sprig floral design and dark green leaves outlined in magenta. **$45.00 – 50.00.**

Plate 78. Waste bowl, 3¼"h, 6"d, soft paste, unmarked, sprig pattern of small green leaves and dots on thin pink branches. **$25.00 – 30.00.**

Plate 79. Cake plate, 9"d, soft paste, unmarked, sprig pattern in a feather or plume design. **$35.00 – 40.00.**

Plate 80. Tea pot, 6½"h, 12"w, soft paste with a pearl ware glaze, unmarked. The sprig pattern is accented with dark blue dots. **$115.00 – 135.00.**

Plate 81. Sugar bowl, 6"h, soft paste, unmarked. $100.00 – 125.00 (mc).

Plate 82. Pitcher, 5"h, soft paste, unmarked. A dark green and magenta flower and branch design is accented with a cobalt blue shape, perhaps an insect. Note the leaves in relief on the lower body, handle, and base. $30.00 – 35.00.

Plate 83. Cake plate, porcelain, Bridgwood & Son impressed mark, see Godden Mark 591, circa mid-1800s. A tiny pink and green sprig pattern alternates with a larger design around the outer border and also appears in the center of the piece. $35.00 – 40.00.

Plate 84. Cups and saucers featuring different sprig patterns, unmarked, circa mid-1800s. $50.00 – 55.00 each.

Plate 85. Sweetmeat dish, 11½"l, porcelain, Derby mark in red, circa 1810, see Godden Mark 1253. An enameled sprig pattern in dark blue, pink, and yellow-gold scattered over surface, gilded border. $500.00 – 600.00.

Plate 86. Sauce boat matching sweetmeat dish and marked the same. The gilded decoration includes leaf designs on the exterior and interior of the spout. $225.00 – 275.00.

Other Early Enamel Floral Patterns

Plate 87. Sparrow beak creamer, 2¾"h, unmarked, circa 1780. The flowers are sprig form in a garland around the interior border and interspersed with a rather crude dot pattern painted over in a dark pink. **$250.00 – 275.00.**

Plate 88. Handleless cup and saucer, attributed to Lowenstoft, circa 1770, decorated similarly to the preceding creamer, but with a large pink rose in the center of the saucer and on the body of the cup. **$275.00 – 325.00.**

Plate 89. Handleless cup and saucer, attributed to the Worcester factory. The molded body design is known as "Worcester Swirl," circa 1800. **$200.00 – 250.00.**

Plate 90. Plate, 7"d, unmarked, circa early to mid-1800s, enameled, "Strawberry" pattern. **$150.00 – 175.00.**

Plate 91. Cup and saucer, unmarked, circa 1820, enamel floral pattern composed of large round pink flowers alternating with a yellow and brown design over a cream-colored glaze. A tea pot and covered sugar bowl in this pattern are shown in the following photographs. **$125.00 – 150.00.**

Plate 92. Tea pot matching cup and saucer. **$425.00 – 475.00.**

Plate 93. Sugar bowl with cover. **$180.00 – 200.00.**

Plate 94. Handleless cup and saucer, unmarked, circa 1810, overglaze pink enamel floral pattern with large green leaves. **$200.00 – 250.00.**

Plate 95. Cup and saucer and plate, unmarked, circa 1840, tulip-shaped floral pattern and green heart shaped leaves. **$150.00 – 175.00.**

Plate 96. Handleless cup and saucer, unmarked, circa 1815, enameled pink roses and blue flowers with yellow centers form a border pattern on both pieces. **$150.00 – 175.00.**

Gaudy Decorations

Gaudy decoration describes vivid polychrome colors used to decorate china from about 1820 until the mid-1800s. The gaudy colors reflect the influence of the Japanese "Imari" wares which were painted with cobalt blue and red-orange. Gaudy Dutch and Gaudy Welsh compose two collecting categories of gaudy decoration. Gaudy Dutch was popular from about 1810 until 1830. Primitive floral designs were large and bold, and the heavy application of cobalt blue contributed to the term "gaudy."

Gaudy Welsh originated in Swansea, Wales, but the style was used by English potters as well. Gaudy Welsh most closely relates to Imari decoration because it used cobalt blue as an underglaze color with a burnt-orange color overglaze in the Japanese manner. The cobalt blue is usually applied in panels. Gaudy Welsh also is characterized by the addition of copper lustre to the decoration.

The cobalt blue of Gaudy Dutch was applied over the glaze. Other colors, such as black, can be found on some china decorated in a gaudy style. While gaudy decoration was handpainted, sometimes the colors were applied over transfer designs. The application of dark paint over a colored transfer design also reinforced the term "gaudy," because the paint obscured the lines of the design, resulting in a colorful but uneven look. Gaudy decorations are generally unmarked. The china bodies are usually simple earthenwares, but ironstone china was decorated in the gaudy style as well, and collectors consider Gaudy Ironstone as another collecting category.

Plate 97. Coffee can, 3"h; pitcher, 6"h, and creamer, 4"h, earthenware, unmarked, circa 1830. The Gaudy Dutch "Oyster" pattern is defined by the large three-section rounded design painted in cobalt blue. **Coffee can, $175.00 – 200.00; Pitcher, $250.00 – 275.00; Creamer, $200.00 – 225.00.**

Plate 98. Tea pot, 7"h, octagonal form, earthenware, circa 1830. The "Oyster" pattern complements an Oriental style building and stylized floral designs. The cobalt blue, burnt-orange, and green enamels are accented with gold. $400.00 – 450.00.

Plate 99. Milk jug, 4¾"h, earthenware, unmarked, circa 1830, Gaudy Dutch "Oyster" pattern. $185.00 – 200.00.

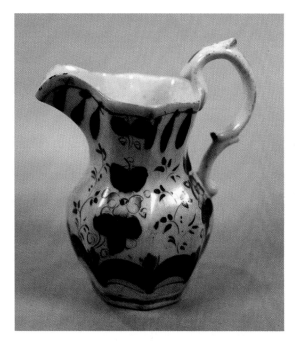

Plate 100. Creamer, 4½"h, earthenware, unmarked, circa 1830, lightly scalloped border with a curved handle. The Gaudy Dutch floral pattern has a very heavy application of cobalt blue. $200.00 – 225.00.

Plate 101. Mush cup, 4"h x 5"d, earthenware, unmarked, circa 1830, decorated with an Oriental floral pattern in a light orange transfer overlaid with cobalt blue, burnt-orange, and green on a white ground. **$75.00 – 100.00.**

Plate 102. Saucer matching preceding mush cup.

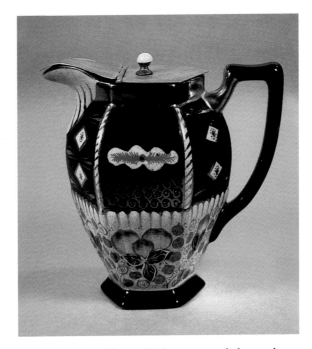

Plate 103. Jug, 7"h, earthenware, unmarked, circa 1820 – 1860. The underglaze cobalt blue panels and copper lustre highlights identify this piece as Gaudy Welsh. **$250.00 – 275.00.**

Plate 104. Pitcher, 6½"h, pewter lid, earthenware, unmarked, circa 1820 – 1860, Gaudy Welsh. **$175.00 – 200.00.**

Lustre Decoration

English lustre decorations date from the late eighteenth century through the mid-nineteenth century, and some companies continued to decorate in that manner during the twentieth century. Examples shown here include pieces from various eras. The lustre wares are usually unmarked unless they are from the later periods. Examples shown include copper and pink lustre. The last three examples are of "Strawberry Lustre," a sub-category of pink lustre wares which incorporates various strawberry-like motifs with pink lustre.

Plate 105. Pitcher, 6"h, unmarked, circa 1880, copper lustre finish on interior and exterior, with a wide black band border overlaid with a silver lustre design at the top of the piece. **$60.00 – 75.00.**

Plate 106. Child's mug, 2½"h, unmarked, circa 1800, copper lustre finish on the exterior and inner border. A wide band in blue enamel enhances the decoration. **$50.00 – 60.00.**

Plate 107. Pitcher, 4"h, unmarked, circa 1800, copper lustre finish on interior and exterior with a wide band of light blue around the top decorated with a simple floral design in copper lustre. **$50.00 – 65.00.**

Plate 108. Pitcher, 4"h, a pink lustre finish on the mid section and interior has been combined with silver lustre patterns and finish on the top half and base. **$35.00 – 45.00.**

Plate 109. Sugar bowl (without lid), white ironstone decorated with a thin outline of leaves in copper lustre, W. & E. Corn. **$60.00 – 75.00 (mc)**

W. & E. Corn mark on sugar bowl, circa 1864 – 1890.

Alfred Meakin mark on platter, circa 1891 – 1897.

Plate 110. Platter, white ironstone, copper lustre "Tea Leaf" pattern, Alfred Meakin. **$225.00 – 250.00.**

Plate 111. Gravy boat, 8"l and underplate, 8¼"l, copper lustre "Tea Leaf" pattern, Wedgwood & Co. **$165.00 – 185.00.**

Wedgwood & Co. mark on gravy boat, circa 1891 – 1906.

Bailey & Harvey impressed mark on pink lustre plate, circa 1834 – 1835.

Plate 112. Plate, 7"d, a large orange enameled flower in the center is highlighted by pink lustre leaves on a lighter pink lustre ground around the wide border, Bailey & Harvey. **$85.00 – 100.00.**

Plate 113. Handleless cup and saucer, unmarked, pink lustre with multi-colored enameled flowers around inner borders. **$125.00 – 150.00.**

Plate 114. Handleless cup and cup plate, unmarked, circa early to mid-1800s, enameled fruit and leaves with pink lustre trim. **$75.00 – 100.00.**

Plate 115. Cake plate with cup and saucer, "Strawberry Lustre" pattern, attributed to Wedgwood, circa 1900. **Cake plate, $175.00 – 225.00; Cup and saucer, $140.00 – 165.00.**

Plate 116. Tea pot matching preceding pieces. $350.00 – 400.00.

Plate 117. Pitcher, 6"h, unmarked, circa 1850, "Strawberry Lustre" pattern decorates top border above a blue enameled body. $150.00 – 175.00.

Chapter Four
 # Oriental Decorative
Themes and Patterns

Oriental motifs influenced English ceramic decoration from the early eighteenth century. English potters imitated or copied original designs found on the underglaze blue and white porcelain which was being imported from China at that time. During that early period, the English patterns were applied with a transfer outline over the glaze of the body of the china and then the outline was filled in with colored enamels. Usually the designs were painted with several different colors. The G.M. & C.J. Mason factory decorated their famous ironstone china in that manner during the early 1800s. Other factories soon followed their example.

Although the Chinese porcelain exhibited underglaze decoration, the English potters were not able to replicate that technique until the nineteenth century, with most companies using the process from the mid-1800s. The English potters had been using the transfer method of decoration from the 1760s, but always overglaze. In this chapter, both methods of decoration, overglaze and underglaze, are illustrated for the Oriental themes.

"Chinoiserie" has evolved as a collector term to describe Oriental designs. Another term associated with Oriental patterns is "Imari" or "Japan Colors." Basically, Imari refers to brightly colored wares made in Japan and exported from the Japanese port of Imari. The Imari or Japan Colors were typified by a dark underglaze cobalt blue and highlighted with a burnt-orange enamel over the glaze. The orange may also be called "iron red," or "India red." Other colored enamels such as yellow, gold, and green were also used in addition to the orange. The Chinese also adapted this style of decoration as well as the English. In Chapter 3, Gaudy decoration was discussed which was based on the Imari style.

Other polychromed Oriental designs used cobalt blue as a base color, but colors other than burnt-orange were incorporated into the pattern. Polychromed Oriental themes are also found without cobalt blue. Magenta, dark red, and black were also dominant colors in overglaze decoration. From the mid to late 1800s, the entire multicolored pattern could be printed underglaze. Consequently, even more Oriental polychrome patterns were produced. Pattern names are not usually found on the early polychromed Oriental designs. References about specific factories sometimes make it possible to identify many of these by a particular name. Other names have been coined over time by collectors.

Certain other identifiable features also distinguish Oriental designs. Figures are easy to recognize because of their dress and hair styles. They are quite frequently shown carrying a parasol. Pagoda-style tea houses, dome roofed structures, and rivers with sampans are often part of the design. Interior room settings feature Oriental furnishings of low tables and chests. Vases with a stylized floral arrangement are a common component of Oriental patterns.

This selection of Oriental decoration on English china is by no means comprehensive. It serves as a colorful glimpse of what is available for collectors. This chapter is sub-divided into (1) examples of multicolored or polychromed Oriental patterns from various factories, with a concentration on the Mason Company and its successors, and (2) monochrome underglaze Oriental patterns made by a number of factories. The monochrome examples are primarily blue and white and include "Flow Blue" patterns and the popular "Blue Willow" pattern. "Mulberry," however, is also represented as well as a few other colors.

Oriental Polychrome Decoration

Various Manufacturers 1800 – 1820s

Plate 118. Creamer, footed waste bowl, and covered sugar bowl, earthenware; polychrome enamels over pink transfer Oriental pattern: a seated woman reading to two children and a teahouse compose the primary scene. Applied rams' heads form handles on sugar bowl; unmarked, circa 1810. **Creamer & sugar, $425.00 – 475.00; Waste bowl, $250.00 – 275.00.**

Plate 119. Jug, 6"h, stone china, cobalt blue border with burnt-orange and bright blue enamels decorate body. The pattern is distinguished by a large light blue flower. An ornate handle in the shape of a serpent's head curves to a split at the base terminating in splayed claw feet; impressed mark of an "X" in a circle with impressed "IRONSTONE CHINA," unidentified factory, circa 1800. **$800.00 – 1,000.00.**

Derby painted mark in red on Imari plate, circa 1800 – 1825.

Plate 120. Plate, 8¼"d, porcelain, polychrome floral pattern in Imari colored enamels on a white ground. The border is distinguished by reserves outlined in cobalt blue, and the outer border is gilded, Derby. **$150.00 – 175.00.**

Plate 121. Coffee cans, porcelain; basic Imari colors of cobalt blue and burnt-orange decorate flower and leaf designs on these pieces. Gold accents all the patterns as well as the rims and handles; attributed to New Hall, circa early 1800s. **$200.00 – 225.00 each.**

Hicks & Meigh printed mark in mauve: coat of arms with "Stone China," circa 1806 – 1822. Note a number (possibly a pattern number) has been crossed out and another "154" substituted.

Plate 122. Plate, 8¾"d, stone china; a mauve floral transfer pattern is accented with dark purple and lavender; the design is distinguished by a zig-zagged fence in the foreground; the scalloped rim is outlined in gold, and gold highlights the cobalt blue leaves around the border; Hicks & Meigh. **$125.00 – 175.00.**

Plate 123. Waste bowl, earthenware; magenta-colored transfer figural pattern: one figure is holding a parasol and a child is holding a bird; green, blue, and yellow enamels with gold lustre; unmarked, circa 1810. **$275.00 – 325.00.**

Plate 124. Mug, 2½"h, earthenware; the same magenta-colored transfer featured on the preceding waste bowl decorates this mug. Note that no other color has been added to the magenta transfer of the child holding the bird; cobalt blue glaze painted on body of mug with handle and bottom rim undecorated; pink lustre frames pattern, rim, and lower border; the application of the cobalt blue and lustre is quite uneven; unmarked; circa 1820. **$150.00 – 175.00.**

John & William Ridgway printed mark in blue, circa 1814 – 1830.

Plate 125. Plate, 10"d, a multicolored Oriental floral pattern in center of plate is surrounded by a pale blue border; cobalt blue designs accent pattern; John & William Ridgway. **$165.00 – 185.00.**

Mayer & Newbold printed initials, "M & N," with "Opaque China," circa 1817 – 1833.

Plate 126. Pitcher, 5½"h, earthenware; the Oriental pattern is enameled in rust-orange, cobalt blue, green, and yellow. Two figures, a small boat, and several houses can be seen in the pattern; the spout of the piece is molded in the shape of a face and is referred to as a "Mask" spout. Mayer & Newbold. **$200.00 – 250.00.**

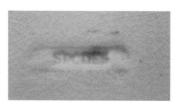

Spode impressed mark, "SPODES NEW STONE" ("New Stone" is only barely visible below name); mark in use between 1805 – 1820.

Plate 127. Plate, 8"d, stone china; Spode's "Bang Up" pattern, circa 1819; a burnt-orange floral transfer decoration overlaid in cobalt blue, burnt-orange, and bright blue; gold accents center flower. **$150.00 – 200.00.**

Spode printed mark in cobalt blue: "Spode's Imperial;" mark in use 1805 – 1833.

Plate 128. Oblong handled dish, 10"l, earthenware; pierced handles with gold accents; Spode's "Frog" pattern, circa 1820; wide outer floral border enameled in cobalt blue and burnt-orange; multicolors of cobalt blue, burnt-orange, and bright blue, highlighted with gold, form a center pattern on a white ground; a piece of stemmed fruit, a small dish with a spoon, and a vase are part of the center design. **$250.00 – 300.00.**

DAVENPORT impressed mark with anchor. A "2" is visible on the left side of the anchor, but the number on the right side is not clear; circa 1820s.

Plate 129. Plate, 9½"d, earthenware; the center blue transfer pattern is overlaid with orange and rose enamels; the pattern features a large urn of flowers sitting on a brick wall; fruits and flowers in similar colors with the addition of yellow form the border; this particular piece was described by tag as "clobbered," another term used to describe polychromed decoration over a transfer; Davenport. **$200.00 – 250.00.**

Plate 130. Cup and saucer, earthenware; an Oriental style floral design featuring a vase and flowers in pink, rust-orange, blue, green, and yellow enamels on a white ground covers body of cup and saucer; unmarked, circa 1820. **$100.00 – 120.00.**

Plate 131. Dish, bone china; Oriental scene of a house, willow tree, and fence, all outlined in gold with overlays of cobalt blue and burnt-orange; New Hall printed mark (Godden Mark 2875) in brown, circa 1812 – 1835. **$100.00 – 120.00.**

Plate 132. Cup and saucer, earthenware; blue transfer scene of two figures in a tea house and one in the garden standing in front of a zigzagged fence; the outer floral border is accented with butterflies; the pattern is overlaid with pastel multicolored enamels; unmarked, circa 1820. **$75.00 – 100.00.**

Mason

The Mason Company's influence on the Staffordshire pottery industry is represented not only by the ironstone ceramic body it developed, but also by its colorful Oriental decorations. Marks and examples follow for the factory and its successors. The G.M. and C.J. Mason Company was in business between 1813 and 1829. Charles James Mason & Co. succeeded that earlier firm from 1829 until 1845. In 1845, Charles James Mason & Co. was declared bankrupt, but the company was continued from 1845 until 1848 and then from 1851 until 1854 under the name of Charles James Mason (see Godden, 1964, p. 419). Meanwhile, Francis Morley purchased the designs and molds of the Charles James Mason Company when it declared bankruptcy in 1845. Morley took over the company in 1852. G.L. Ashworth was associated with Francis Morely from 1858 until 1862, at which time Ashworth became the owner of the factory under the name of G.L. Ashworth Bros.

During this long period of time, the same or similar Mason marks were used. Thus Mason marks can be confusing. There are several ways in which the marks can be linked to specific time periods. The G.M. and C.J. Mason Company operated from 1813 until 1829. The early Mason marks were impressed and consisted of "Masons Patent Ironstone" written either in a circular or linear style from 1813 until 1825. A printed crown mark was initiated in 1820. The crown had a rounded top. The name "Mason's" was not printed above the crown when that mark was first implemented. This printed crown mark often accompanies the impressed marks. When the company name changed to Charles James Mason & Co., the printed crown mark was continued with "Mason's" printed over the crown. "Mason's" printed over the crown, however, appears to have been initiated before 1829. A variation of the "Patent Ironstone China" mark printed within the drape under the crown with "Improved Ironstone China" was instituted during the 1840s. The shape of the crown appears more angular than round in that particular mark, see Godden Mark 2534.

When the company name changed to Charles James Mason (without "& Co.") in 1845, the shape of the crown was changed to a definite square shape on each side (see marks). The rounded top crown, however, was also continued for some time after 1845. From 1845 until 1854, several versions of the printed crown mark were used, with either rounded or angular tops and with "Mason's" printed above the crown and "Patent Ironstone China" printed within a drape beneath the crown. These crown marks are noted to have been continued when Francis Morley took over the company in 1852. Eventually "F. Morley & Co." was printed above the crown. In 1862, when G.L. Ashworth & Sons succeeded Morley, the squared-off version of the printed crown mark was continued. The name "Mason's" continued to be printed over the crown, but at some point after 1862, "Ashworth's" was also printed beneath the drape. After 1891, "England" was added beneath the drape mark. The squared-off crown mark, thus, could be as early as the mid to late 1840s or as late as 1890, if "Ashworth's" or "England" is not also printed with the mark (see Godden, 1964, pgs. 416 – 418).

G.M. & C.J. Mason Marks and Examples 1813 – 1829

One of the following marks used by G.M. & C.J. Mason is found on the pieces in this section. The particular mark is described in the caption of the photograph. A few examples have two marks, an impressed and a printed mark. Dating periods for each mark are noted.

Mark a, Mason's impressed circular mark: MASON'S PATENT IRONSTONE CHINA, circa 1813 – 1825.

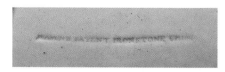

Mark b, Mason's impressed linear mark: MASON'S PATENT IRONSTONE CHINA, circa 1813 – 1825.

Mark c, Mason's printed crown and drape mark in black without the name "MASON'S" printed above crown, circa from 1820. See Godden explanation for Godden Mark

Mark d, Mason's printed crown and drape mark in mauve with the name "MASON'S" printed above crown, circa after 1820.

Mark e, Mason's printed "FENTON STONE WORKS," in blue, circa 1825.

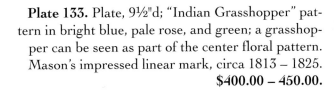

Mark f, Mason's printed "Fenton Stone Works," with "No 306" printed below the mark. Godden notes that this number refers to the pattern (Godden: 1964, p. 418, Mark 2541). The same number may also be found on other patterns.

Plate 133. Plate, 9½"d; "Indian Grasshopper" pattern in bright blue, pale rose, and green; a grasshopper can be seen as part of the center floral pattern. Mason's impressed linear mark, circa 1813 – 1825. **$400.00 – 450.00.**

Plate 134. Teapot stand, 7¾"d, octagonal shape; the design on this piece is referred to as Mason's "Japan" pattern. Cobalt blue, a bright blue, and burnt-orange are the basic colors painted on this floral pattern on a white ground. This pattern is typified by three large open blossom flowers with the center one overlaid in deep cobalt blue. Mason's circular impressed mark, circa 1813 – 1825. **$350.00 – 400.00.**

Plate 135. Covered sauce tureen, 8"l; Mason's "Japan" pattern; the primary cobalt blue flower of the pattern is outlined in gold, and its center is painted gold also; cobalt handles and finials are accented in gold. Mason's impressed linear mark, circa 1813 – 1825. $1,200.00 – 1,400.00.

Plate 136. Plate, 8"d; burnt-orange flowers scattered randomly over surface with cobalt blue leaves painted on a white ground; a small fence outlined in cobalt blue is in the foreground with a splotch of green enamel representing grass. These colors, burnt-orange and cobalt blue, are referred to as "Japan Colors" by Mason collectors. "Japan Colors," however, are not to be confused with Mason's "Japan" pattern (see preceding photographs). Although the "Japan" pattern incorporates Japan colors, it is a separate pattern from the many others which are painted in those distinctive shades. Mason's impressed linear mark, circa 1813 – 1825. $350.00 – 400.00.

Plate 137. Shallow bowl, 8½"d; polychrome floral center and border pattern in Japan Colors separated by an inner cobalt blue border punctuated with pink roses in four reserves. A large burnt-orange flower is the focus of the center pattern. Mason's impressed linear mark, circa 1813 – 1825. $300.00 – 400.00.

Plate 138. Soup bowl, 9½"d; "Scroll Chinoiserie" pattern, multicolored enamels in pastel shades are overlaid on this Oriental figural pattern featuring a seated male with three females in a garden setting; the floral border is accented by reserves at the top and bottom containing fancy scrolls. Mason's impressed linear mark (1813 – 1825) with Mason's printed crown and drape mark (1825 – 1829). **$300.00 – 375.00 (mc).**

Plate 139. Plate, 8"d; "Water Lily" pattern in Japan Colors; a large water lily dominates the center pattern. Mason's impressed linear mark, circa 1813 – 1825. **$275.00 – 325.00.**

Plate 140. Drainer, 12¼"l x 9"w; "Water Lily" pattern in Japan Colors; Mason's impressed linear mark written in two lines rather than one, circa 1813 – 1825. **$1,000.00 – 1,200.00.**

Plate 141. Platter, 11"l; Oriental scenic pattern polychromed in Japan Colors. A plant with large cobalt blue leaves accented in gold is on the left with a zig-zagged fence; a flowering tree is on the right side. A dagger type border separates the outer and inner borders. Mason's printed crown and drape mark, circa 1820. **$350.00 – 400.00.**

Plate 142. Cake plate with scalloped handles; Oriental floral pattern featuring a large zig-zagged fence in the foreground; Japan Colors overlay the design on a white ground; Mason's printed "Fenton Stone Works" mark in blue with number "306," circa 1825. **$175.00 – 225.00.**

Plate 143. Pitcher, 7"h; note the similarities in the elements of this body pattern and the preceding border pattern. The body of the serpent forming the handle is painted in a light green while the head is painted in a pale orange lustre which is repeated around the outer rim and in a border around the top third of the pitcher. Mason's printed "Fenton Stone Works" mark in blue with the number "306," circa 1825. **$375.00 – 425.00.**

Plate 144. Plate, 9½"d; "Flower Pot and Table" pattern, a large vase and a round table with a fancy pedestal compose the primary features of this Oriental design painted in a number of different colors with pink and dark green dominant; Mason's impressed linear mark with the printed crown and drape mark, circa 1820 – 1829. **$300.00 – 350.00.**

Plate 145. Platter, 12½"l, rectangular, paneled shape; "Flower Pot and Table" pattern, marked the same as the preceding example. **$500.00 – 600.00.**

Plate 146. Plate, 8"d, "Mogul" Oriental figural pattern: three figures, one with a parasol, and a large vase on the left side compose the design. The pattern is overlaid with cobalt blue, deep yellow, greens, pinks, and rust-orange enamels; unmarked, attributed to Mason's, circa 1818 – 1820. **$300.00 – 350.00.**

Charles James Mason & Co. 1829 – 1845/Charles James Mason 1845 – 1848 & 1851 – 1854

Mark a, printed crown and drape mark in brown with "MASON'S" printed above crown, circa after 1829, Charles James Mason & Co.

Mark b, printed crown and drape mark in brown with "Mason's" printed above crown, circa 1845 and after, Charles James Mason. Note the more angular shape of the crown in this mark from the one in Mark a.

Plate 147. Pitcher, 5¾"; "Bandana" pattern; transfers of dragons and flowers form an overall pattern on body with the top half overlaid in black and the bottom half overlaid in burnt-orange. The dragons are heavily outlined in black, and several other colors highlight the floral designs on the top half of the pitcher. Charles James Mason printed crown and drape mark in black, circa after 1845. $300.00 – 400.00.

Plate 148. Compote, 7"h, 13¼"w, this polychrome Oriental scenic center pattern featuring tea houses and small mountains is called the "Chinese Mountain" pattern. Burnt-orange is the predominant color on the wide outer border. Gold scrolled work accents the piece. Charles James Mason & Co. printed crown and drape mark in brown, circa 1830 – 1835. $800.00 – 1,000.00.

Plate 149. Pitcher, 5¼"h; "Double Landscape" pattern (only part of the pattern is visible); overlapping reserves of a mountain and water scene are the basis for the name of this pattern; the reserves are surrounded by a burnt-orange background which in turn is on a very deep cobalt blue finish accented with gold designs; the handle has a light blue tint. Charles James Mason & Co. printed crown and drape mark in brown, circa 1829 – 1845. **$1,100.00 – 1,200.00.**

Plate 150. Pitcher, 5½"h, an Oriental figural pattern painted in multicolors forms a reserve on the front of this piece. Three men are in a garden with one figure seated and the other two standing. The surrounding background is painted with Japan Colors with the primary design composed of scale work in a deep red; hence the name of the pattern is Mason's "Red Scale" pattern; Charles James Mason & Co. printed crown and drape mark in black, circa 1829 – 1845. **$600.00 – 700.00.**

Plate 151. Covered bowl, 11"d x 6½"h; "Rich Ruby" pattern in Japan Colors with gold scroll work on pattern, handles, and finial. The center pattern is an urn filled with multicolored flowers on a white ground. A combination of birds and flowers in light to dark shades of orange on a cobalt blue ground forms the border pattern. The petal-shaped finial has a spot of olive green paint in its center. Charles James Mason & Co. printed crown and drape mark in brown, circa 1829 – 1845. **$600.00 – 700.00.**

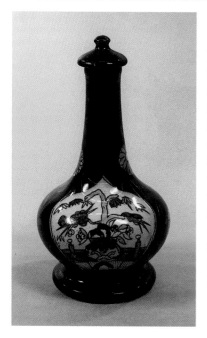

Plate 152. Perfume bottle, 4½"h; a dark cobalt blue finish on body frames a polychrome Oriental floral pattern on a white ground; unmarked, attributed to Charles James Mason & Co., circa 1835. **$800.00 – 1,000.00.**

Plate 153. Sucrier (sugar bowl), 6"h x 9"w; floral pattern overlaid with Japan Colors and gold accents; unmarked, attributed to Charles James Mason & Co., circa 1835 – 1845. **$300.00 – 400.00.**

Plate 154. Plate, 6¾"d; a vase containing a large spray of flowers displayed on a dining table (note chair backs at table) composes the center pattern of this design which is painted in Japan Colors on a white ground. The wide border is fashioned with cameos of a large pale orange bird. Flowers, painted in gold on cobalt blue reserves which blend into the border, alternate with the bird cameos. This pattern is like Mason's Rich Ruby except for the color of the large flower in the vase. Charles James Mason's printed crown and drape mark in brown, circa 1845 and after. **$100.00 – 120.00.**

Plate 155. Dessert dish, 10¼"l x 8¼"w; cobalt blue and burnt-orange color this Oriental floral pattern on a white ground. Two long cobalt blue leaves accented with gold designs distinguish the center floral arrangement which is in a round vase on a low table. The wide cobalt blue border is broken by insets of scrolled work in shades of orange. Charles James Mason's printed crown and drape mark in brown, circa 1845 and after. **$450.00 – 550.00.**

G.L. Ashworth Marks and Examples 1862 – 1890

Mark a, Impressed name mark, "Ashworth," circa 1862 – 1880.

Mark b, Printed coat of arms mark with "Real Ironstone China" printed in a circle surrounding the coat of arms; "G.L. ASHWORTH & BROS. HANLEY" printed below, circa 1862 – 1880.

Mark c, Ashworth's printed mark incorporating Mason's crown and drape mark, after 1862.

Mark e, Ashworth Bros. printed Mason's crown and drape mark with "MASON'S" printed above crown and "ENGLAND" printed below drape, after 1891.

Mark d, Ashworth Bros. printed crown mark with "ASHWORTH'S" printed above crown and "Hanley" printed in a banner below crown, after 1880.

Plate 156. Plate 9"d, "Aurora" pattern; the center pattern is composed of fancy scroll work in black and slate gray with one large burnt-orange flower as the focal point; the border pattern has a similar scrolled design with leaves painted a yellow-gold; Ashworth Bros. printed crown mark in blue, circa after 1880. $75.00 – 100.00.

Plate 157. Plate, 8¾"d, octagonal shape; "Bandana" pattern, an earlier Mason design; impressed Ashworth mark, circa 1862 – 1880. **$275.00 – 325.00.**

Plate 158. Jug, 4½"h; "Bandana" pattern; Ashworth's printed Mason's crown and drape mark in black, after 1862. **$350.00 – 450.00.**

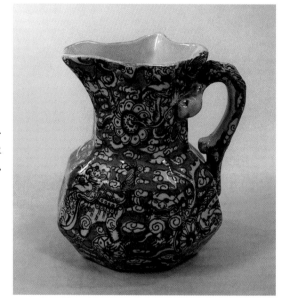

Plate 159. Plate, 7½"; "Bandana" pattern over surface of a plate framing center reserve of an Oriental figural scene with a person seated by an open window; Ashworth impressed mark, circa 1862 – 1880. **$125.00 – 150.00.**

Plate 160. Chowder cups, 2¾"h x 5½"d, and saucers, 7"d; "Bible" pattern; multi-colored flowers in orange, yellow-gold, blue, and green on a cream-colored ground form a center and border pattern; Ashworth's printed Mason's crown and drape mark in brown with "England" under drape, circa after 1891. **$100.00 – 150.00 each.**

Plate 161. Trivet, 6¼"d; "Double Landscape" pattern; Oriental scenic water and land pattern in two overlapping squares is the basis for the name of this design which is composed of a mauve transfer overlaid with numerous colors dominated by a dark green; Ashworth impressed mark, circa 1862 – 1880. **$250.00 – 300.00.**

Plate 162. Plate, 9"d; "Double Landscape" pattern; this rendition of the pattern is in Japan Colors and the ground is overlaid with dark cobalt blue; Ashworth's printed Mason's crown and drape mark in black, after 1862. **$350.00 – 400.00.**

Plate 163. Teapot, 5½"h; "Old Japan Vase" pattern colored in burnt-orange and black; a vase on a table is the dominant feature of the design; unmarked, attributed to Ashworth, circa 1862. **$275.00 – 325.00.**

Plate 164. Chamber pot, 5¾"h x 9"w, serpent-shaped handle; "Peking Japan" pattern; black scenic transfer design portraying a large Oriental style house painted with burnt-orange, blue, and green; Ashworth's black printed Mason's crown and drape mark, circa 1862. **$300.00 – 350.00.**

Plate 165. Plate, 7¼"d; "Pekoe" pattern; the slate gray transfer pattern is highlighted with dark orange and touches of light green; a large bird and flowering tree compose the center pattern which only has very light touches of color; three floral sprays decorate the border; Ashworth Bros. printed crown mark with "HANLEY" and "ENGLAND" plus the pattern name "PEKOE" with "W583," circa 1891 – 1900. **$60.00 – 75.00.**

Plate 166. Pitcher, 6"h; "Persiana" pattern; the mauve transfer floral design is overlaid with vivid colors of blue, orange, yellow, and green on a white ground; Ashworth's printed Mason's crown and drape mark in red with "PERSIANA" and "ENGLAND" printed below mark, after 1891. **$120.00 – 140.00.**

Plate 167. Tea set, "Red Scale" pattern; Oriental figural scenes form reserves for the red scale background. Notice the plates which only have a small circle of the red scale pattern framing the figural scene; Ashworth's black printed Mason's crown and drape mark, circa 1890. **$1,400.00 – 1,600.00 set.**

Plate 168. Jug, 7¾"h, octagonal shape; Oriental scenic pattern in multicolors cover body; a teahouse, a boat, and birds are part of the pattern; black scroll work around top border on interior and exterior; Ashworth's black printed Mason's crown and drape mark with "ENGLAND" below, circa after 1891. **$275.00 – 300.00.**

Plate 169. Plate, 10¼"d; a stylized leaf design in orange and green forms a center reserve on a white ground; black transfers of floral designs have been left undecorated and are highlighted by a dark top border on interior and exterior; Ashworth's black printed Mason's crown and drape mark, circa 1862 – 1880 with an impressed mark of "Real Ironstone China." **$275.00 – 300.00.**

Plate 170. Plate, 7¾"d; Oriental floral pattern in shades of rose and blue; a jardiniere is on the right side of the design, and large flowers cover the surface with only a small break between the border and center pattern; the bottom half of the center design is highlighted with a pale orange; Ashworth's printed coat of arms mark, circa 1862 – 1880. **$75.00 – 100.00.**

Plate 171. Plate, 8"d; two vases, one in dark green and the other in a light peach, are the focal points of the center pattern; shades of pink, yellow, and green color the flowers in the design. The border design is ornate with floral and scroll work in white highlighted by burnt-orange and dark green; Ashworth's printed Mason's crown and drape mark with "England," after 1891. **$100.00 – 125.00.**

Various Factories 1830 – 1860s

Plate 172. Soup tureen with underplate; "Chusan" pattern in cobalt blue, burnt-orange, and peach over a tinted pale blue ground accompanied by gold outlining and scroll work. The pattern contains the components of a room with urns of flowers and Oriental furnishings. William Ridgway & Co. printed royal arms mark in mauve with "IRONSTONE CHINA, CHU-SAN," circa 1830 – 1854. **$650.00 – 750.00.**

Plate 173. Dessert stand; floral pattern overlaid in Japan Colors over a white ground; "Pearl" impressed mark, attributed to John Ridgway, circa 1830; **$350.00 – 400.00.**

Impressed Minton mark with mauve printed mark, "M & Co." and pattern name "MONA," circa 1841 – 1873.

Plate 174. Dessert plate, 7"d; "Mona" floral pattern; multicolored enamels over a mauve transfer design on a white ground; a vase of flowers, a basket of flowers, and a bird decorate the center and inner border of the piece; a narrow outer border diaper pattern is punctuated by small diamond shapes, Minton. **$55.00 – 70.00.**

F. Morley & Co. printed crown mark in blue with "F. Morley & Co." above crown, circa 1845 – 1858.

Plate 175. Plate, 10¼"d; cobalt blue, burnt-orange, and green enamels are overlaid on this transfer pattern; the center design contains a one-handled vase with flowers and an open chest inside an octagonal-shaped frame of cobalt blue; an inner border is composed of burnt-orange flowers and cobalt blue scrolls accented with gold outlining inside a banded outer border of burnt-orange flowers and green leaves. F. Morley & Co. **$175.00 – 200.00.**

F. Morley & Co. impressed mark with printed pattern name "Aurora," circa 1845 – 1858.

Plate 176. Plate, 9"d, Handleless cup, 3"h, and saucer, 6"d; "Aurora" pattern; mauve transfer floral pattern overlaid with dark purple, green, blue, and touches of yellow on a white ground decorates center and border of pieces; F. Morley & Co. **Plate, $150.00 – 175.00; Handleless cup and saucer, $70.00 – 90.00.**

F. Morley & Co. printed mark in mauve: initials "F.M. & Co." under printed pattern name, "California," circa 1845 – 1858.

Plate 177. Plate, 8½"d; "California" pattern; mauve transfer floral design overlaid with purple; a large yellow flower distinguishes the center pattern; the border pattern is highlighted on each side by a large flower accented with pale blue around the outer petals. F. Morley & Co. $75.00 – 125.00.

"IMPROV'D CANTON CHINA" printed mark in blue on covered vegetable dish; factory unidentified, circa 1840 – 1850.

Plate 178. Covered vegetable dish, 12"l, cobalt blue and burnt-orange are the primary colors on this bird and floral pattern which covers the interior of the bowl and surface of the cover; cobalt blue with gold outlining decorates handles and finial; unidentified factory. $400.00 – 500.00.

Unidentified factory, printed pattern mark, "YORK," on pitcher at right, circa 1840 – 1850.

Plate 179. Pitcher, 7"h, "York" pattern; blue transfer floral pattern overlaid with cobalt blue and burnt-orange on a white ground on body and border of pitcher; unidentified factory. **$200.00 – 225.00.**

Plate 180. Platter, 21"l x 17"w, deep well on one end and broad scalloped feet on the other end; Imari colors over a blue transfer pattern decorate this floral and scenic pattern; Oriental buildings are shown in reserves around outer border accented with elaborate scroll work in cobalt blue with burnt-orange flowers and scrolled work; the center pattern incorporates the same colors in a large floral pattern on a white ground; unidentified factory. **$500.00 – 600.00.**

Printed mark on platter, "WARREN 28 DAME STREET, DUBLIN," unidentified factory, mark appears to be a retailer's mark, circa 1840 – 1860.

Underside of platter, showing scalloped feet and deep well.

Plate 181. Bowl, 10"d; a light blue floral transfer floral spray in the center is overlaid with a very light yellow enamel; the three floral sprays around inner border of well have highlights of deeper colors in gold, green, and orange; the inside rim border is decorated with a pattern of single flowers in gold, pink, and orange on a turquoise ground; a narrow band of orange lustre is painted around the inner rim; W.T. Copeland's mark, "COPELAND, LATE SPODE," circa 1847 – 1867. See Godden's mark 1068. **$75.00 – 100.00.**

Plate 182. Oval dish, 10½"l x 7¼"w; floral and bird transfer pattern overlaid with blue, green, burnt-orange, and yellow; two birds, one with colorful plumage, form focal point of pattern. W.T. Copeland's printed mark "SPODE" inside square with "STONE CHINA" printed below, circa 1847 – 1891. This mark is like an earlier mark used by the Spode factory from 1805 – 1830. **$125.00 – 175.00.**

Plate 183. Platter, 17½"l x 13¾"w, octagonal shape; "Amula" pattern; green transfer pattern overlaid with shades of green, mauve, red, blue, and yellow; a large empty vase and a large floral spray form center pattern on a white ground; the wide outer border is decorated with four single flowers painted in red alternating with four floral clusters painted with yellow centers on a dark green ground; "E. CHALLINOR & CO." printed below ribbon with pattern name, "AMULA," in green, circa 1853 – 1862. **$300.00 – 350.00.**

Plate 184. Sauce tureen and underplate; large brown branches with pink flowers and dark green leaves form a border pattern on underplate and decorate the body and lid of the tureen; gold accents on handles, feet, and finial; unmarked, attributed to Pinder, Bourne & Co., circa 1860. **$500.00 – 700.00.**

Plate 185. Platter, 17¾"l x 14½"w; "Apsley Plants" floral pattern; large petal flowers with touches of red and green leaves form center pattern with smaller sprays of flowers around outer border; a very dark application of cobalt blue on one flower and one small leaf in center pattern and on long leaves of floral sprays on border highlights the decoration; the outer border is composed of lightly scrolled designs in blue; gold trim on outer border; Burgess & Leigh printed initials "B. & L." with pattern name, circa 1862 and after. **$500.00 – 700.00.**

Various Factories 1870s – early 1900s

Plate 186. Plate, 9"d; "Bombay" floral pattern; Japan Colors decorate this floral and scroll wide border design; a heavy application of dark cobalt blue has been overlaid on the scroll work and highlights the floral reserves; beaded scalloped edge trimmed in gold; John Maddock & Sons, Ltd., printed crown over circle mark with "Burslem, Staffordshire," circa after 1896. **$45.00 – 60.00.**

Plate 187. Cup and saucer in the Bombay pattern by Maddock. $45.00 – 60.00.

Plate 188. Plate, 9"d; "Canton" floral pattern; a small Oriental style building is on the far right of the center pattern which contains large flowers in dark green, cobalt blue, burnt-orange, and yellow on a white ground encircled by a narrow diaper design in blue; the wide floral border in similar colors is accented by large burnt-orange flowers; Coalport crown mark with "England," after 1891. $45.00 – 60.00.

"Edge, Malkin & Co." impressed name mark with printed initials, "E.M. & Co.., B." under pattern name "CHANG," in blue-green, circa 1871 – 1880.

Plate 189. Plate, 7½"d; "Chang" figural and scenic pattern; two figures in a garden with two urns of flowers compose center pattern; the blue-green transfer is colored with touches of yellow-gold and orange on a white ground; a diaper pattern forms outer border and the rim is trimmed in a dark red-brown; Edge, Malkin & Co.; sometimes this pattern is found in different colors and with a copper lustre border. $30.00 – 40.00.

Plate 190. Plate, 10"d; "Derby Japan" floral pattern; Japan Colors of cobalt blue and burnt-orange decorate flowers; a small floral spray is in the center surrounded by a border of large flowers and stylized cobalt blue "V" shapes; Sampson Hancock impressed initials "S.H." and impressed Registry mark for 1888. **$45.00 – 60.00.**

Doulton printed mark in black with "DRESDEN" and "DOULTON" printed at top and bottom of a circle inside a wreath with a crown above; impressed mark "DOULTON BURSLEM ENGLAND," with an impressed mark of "1-05" for January 1905. Note that the crown and wreath printed mark is like that of Doulton's predecessor, Pinder, Bourne, and Hope, see Godden Mark 3045.

Plate 191. Plate, 7½"d; "Dresden" is the pattern name on this piece, but it is also the popular "Indian Tree" or "Tree of Life" pattern, see following photographs. A stylized tree with flowering branches forms center pattern with large flowers and leaves on inner border; Greek Key designs compose borders around well and outer rim of plate; the blue-gray transfer pattern is highlighted with some black outlining on tree and touches of rose on the flowers in the pattern; Doulton. **$35.00 – 45.00.**

Copeland's printed mark in green of a "C" in square with "SPODE" above and "COPELAND, ENGLAND" below; there is also a retailer's mark of "Soane and Smith" printed in brown, circa after 1891.

Plate 192. Plate, 9½"d; "Indian Tree" pattern; this version of the pattern is brightly colored in rose and green with a gray-black diaper pattern around outer border accenting floral reserves; Copeland. **$50.00 – 65.00.**

Mintons' impressed *fleur-de-lis* year cypher for 1916 and printed crown and globe mark in black.

Plate 193. Plate, 9"d; "Indian Tree" pattern in rose and green with black Greek Key outer border; Mintons, **$50.00 – 65.00.**

Myott, Son & Co. printed crown mark in brown with "IMPERIAL SEMI-PORCELAIN" in two lines above crown and "MYOTT, SON & CO." on either side of crown; "ENGLAND" and "INDI-ANA" below crown, circa 1907.

Plate 194. Plate, 10"d, "Indiana" figural and floral pattern; a pagoda with the figure of a woman visible in the door, and large flowers form the center pattern in a brown transfer highlighted by burnt-orange and cobalt blue; a dark cobalt blue outer border and reserves on the inner border are broken by the floral designs; Myott, Son & Co. $35.00 – 45.00.

Bates, Gildea & Walker printed mark with pattern name "Satsuma," and a registry mark for 1879.

Plate 195. Plate, 10½"d, "Satsuma" pattern, an Oriental floral design in a green transfer; the inner and outer borders are painted orange over the transfer design as is the fan-shaped reserve in the center; Bates, Gildea & Walker. $35.00 – 45.00.

Burgess & Leigh printed globe mark in red-brown with "BURGESS & LEIGH MID-DLEPORT POTTERY BURSLEM" printed in banners around globe; "ENGLAND" printed above globe and "SIAM" pattern name printed below globe, circa 1912.

Plate 196. Platter, 16"l; "Siam" floral pattern; mauve transfer floral design with light orange coloring on flowers and a deep cobalt blue overlaid on the leaves; gilded outer border; Burgess & Leigh. **$225.00 – 250.00.**

Hibbert & Boughey printed mark in blue with initials "H & B" below crown and registry number, circa 1889.

Plate 197. Waste bowl, 3½"h x 6"d; a large floral design encircles body and inner rim of bowl; the pattern is overlaid with dark cobalt blue and burnt-orange. A burnt-orange flower surrounded by cobalt blue leaves on the base is highlighted by two strips of turquoise; Hibbert & Boughey. **$75.00 – 100.00.**

Plate 198. Vase, 10"h; Imari colors decorate this floral and scenic transfer design; a small vase is visible on the body; Oriental style houses are part of the top border pattern; marked "ENGLAND," circa after 1891. **$225.00 – 250.00.**

C A U L D O N impressed mark and printed mark in red of "CAULDON" over "ENGLAND," circa after 1905.

Plate 199. Plate, 10"d; a mauve floral transfer center and border pattern is highlighted by a turquoise outer border and scroll designs; rose is the dominant color of the flowers; Cauldon. **$45.00 – 60.00.**

Mintons' printed crown and globe mark in red with "ENGLAND," circa 1891 – 1902.

Plate 200. Plate, 7½"; mauve transfer floral pattern covers well of plate and extends to outer border; a vase is overlaid with cobalt blue; a compote style vase is on the left side of the design. The pattern is overlaid with brown, yellow, blue, rose, and green enamels, Mintons. **$30.00 – 40.00.**

Plate 201. Mush set: Bowl and pitcher; bright blue, yellow, brown, rose, and green color this floral pattern which covers the surface of the pieces; Mintons' printed crown and globe mark in red with "England," circa 1891 – 1902. **$75.00 – 110.00 for set.**

Ridgway, Sparks & Ridgway impressed Staffordshire knot mark with impressed initials "R.S.R.," circa 1873 – 1879.

Plate 202. Drainer, sauce tureen, and underplate; scrolled designs overlaid in dark cobalt blue surrounding a large flower compose basic pattern. The large flower and other smaller flowers in the pattern are tinted in shades of light to dark orange; gold trim outlines handles and finial; a dark red-brown color trims the edges of the pieces; Ridgway, Sparks & Ridgway. **Drainer, $600.00 – 700.00; Sauce tureen, $600.00 – 700.00; Underplate, $400.00 – 500.00.**

Plate 203. Plate, 10"d; a large vase on a short stand and a small rectangular box form the primary features of this polychromed transfer pattern on a white ground; large flowers and leaves also decorate the center and the inner border; the lightly scalloped outer border is highlighted in yellow-gold; unmarked, circa 1890s. **$45.00 – 60.00.**

Oriental Monochrome Decoration, Late 1700s – Early 1900s

The most popular monochrome color for china decoration is blue. That color is, of course, the one most associated with English china transfer patterns, whether they are Oriental in nature or use some other theme. Historically, blue was the only color which could withstand the high temperatures necessary for firing a pattern under the glaze without running. The process was not known in England until the 1760s, however. During the early 1800s, English potters perfected the method. Techniques improved over the years, and it became possible to use other colors under the glaze. For Oriental patterns, however, blue appears to have continued to be the most popular color. Examples in other colors are not very abundant in comparison. Mulberry was probably the second color most frequently used for Oriental transfers. That color's use on Oriental patterns also has a historical basis, for it was the first color, after blue, to be successfully fired under the glaze. Mulberry was popular from the 1830s through the 1850s. Consequently, many Oriental patterns were made in Mulberry. By the 1840s, other colors including brown, green, and dark pink or red could be used for underglaze transfer patterns.

There are two large collecting areas which are closely associated with blue and white Oriental decoration. One is a specific decorating technique, "Flow Blue." The other is an Oriental pattern, "Blue Willow." I have written separate books on these two subjects, as have others. Consequently, only a few examples of Flow Blue and Blue Willow are included here. Many of the Flow Blue Oriental patterns were also made without being "flowed," and thus the same pattern names can be found on renditions made in other colors.

The following monochrome underglaze transfer Oriental patterns were made by a number of factories. Marks which were on the pieces are shown when available or noted in the captions of the pictures. There are some unmarked examples and some without marked pattern names as well. The china in this section has various body types, ranging from simple earthenware to ironstone or stone china to porcelain. A number of factors are represented, but there are also some examples which remain unidentified as to manufacturer and/or pattern name. The time periods for these illustrated monochrome Oriental patterns also range from the late 1700s through the early 1900s, with most being from the mid to late 1800s. The patterns are arranged in alphabetical order by pattern name. The color of the pattern is blue on white unless noted otherwise. A few examples of Mason's monochrome Oriental patterns are included in this part of the chapter.

Plate 204. "Aladdin," John Ridgway, see Godden Mark 3254, circa 1830 – 1855, lid to covered vegetable dish, paneled shape. The pattern is an Oriental figural water scene. Three people, one playing an instrument, are in a boat in the foreground; a large three-story house is on the right bank and a large willow-type tree is on the left bank. **$100.00 – 125.00.**

Plate 205. "Blue Pheasants," G.M. & C.J. Mason, Mason's circular impressed mark and printed crown and drape mark in blue, circa 1825 – 1829; 16"l, deeply scalloped; Oriental style floral and bird pattern. **$500.00 – 600.00.**

G.M. & C.J. Mason's printed crown and drape mark in blue, from circa 1820.

Plate 206. "Blue Pheasants," chestnut bowl and underplate with reticulated inner borders. **$1,000.00 – 1,200.00.**

"JOHN MADDOCK & SONS ROYAL VITREOUS ENGLAND" printed in red in a circle under a crown with the pattern name, "BOMBAY," printed beneath, circa after 1896.

Plate 207. "Bombay," John Maddock & Sons, red transfer, covered vegetable dish; a figural water scene decorates the interior of the bowl: two women, one seated, with parasols are in the foreground; a boat with a sail is on the left; a fanciful urn held aloft by two figures sits on top of a fence in front of a large house and behind the women. The exterior of the lid and the bowl are decorated with a floral pattern **$75.00 – 125.00.**

Pattern mark on preceding plate: "CHINESE PAGODA AND BRIDGE" printed on ribbons fashioning a fancy knot in blue; unidentified factory, circa early to mid 1800s.

Plate 208. "Chinese Pagoda and Bridge," unidentified factory, plate, scalloped rim; the center pattern features a pagoda surrounded by water; a figure is standing on a bridge in the foreground; large trees are on the right side; reserves with Greek Key designs alternate with flowers on the inner border; a cobalt blue border highlights the inner border. **$75.00 – 100.00 (mc)**

Plate 209. "Chinese Ruins," Davenport, Godden Mark 1181, circa 1795 and after, soup plate, 9¾"d; an Oriental figural pattern portrays one person standing with a parasol and another seated on the ground; a willow tree is on the right; large palm trees are part of both the center and border pattern. The figures are separated by a simple fence from buildings in the background. **$225.00 – 250.00.**

PODMORE, WALKER & CO. printed mark of a bird carrying a banner with "P.W. & Co." printed in lower part and pattern name "COREAN" printed inside banner, circa 1834 – 1859.

Plate 210. "Corean," Podmore, Walker & Co. mulberry transfer, soup bowl, 9¾"d; a fancy fence with a large urn of flowers at one end and a tall willow tree are separated from a pagoda by a river. **$100.00 – 125.00.**

Plate 211. "Corean," pattern in black, platter, 16"l with the same Podmore, Walker & Co. mark as on preceding example. $300.00 – 400.00.

"DAVENPORT" printed at top and bottom of a scrolled cartouche printed with the pattern name "CYPRUS," circa mid 1800s.

Plate 212. "Cyprus," Davenport, mulberry transfer, plate, 9"d, paneled shape; the pattern is composed of a floral border pattern and a center design featuring pagodas, a body of water, and a large palm tree. $100.00 – 125.00.

"T. WALKER" printed above a scrolled cartouche with "IRON-STONE" printed beneath and the pattern name "HONG" printed on the interior, circa 1845 – 1851.

Plate 213. "Hong," T. Walker, mulberry transfer, plate, 9"d; in the foreground of the center pattern, a bridge has steps leading to a pagoda; a flowering tree, entwined with a willow tree in front of the pagoda distinguishes the design. $100.00 – 125.00.

Plate 214. "Jeddo," W. Adams & Sons, mulberry transfer, plate, 9½"d; a large vase, banked by large flowers, dominates the center pattern; a fence, flowering tree, and pagoda are in the background on one side of a river with a large pagoda on the other side; floral designs are spaced around the border. $100.00 – 125.00.

"W. ADAMS & SONS" printed inside a garter mark with a bird above and "IRONSTONE" printed below. The mark is circa 1819 – 1864, but mulberry versions of the pattern would be circa 1840s – 1850s.

"J. MEIR & SON" printed inside double circle with a crown on top; the pattern name "KIR-KEE" is printed inside; "IRON-STONE ENGLAND" is printed below, circa 1890 – 1897.

Plate 215. "KIRKEE," J. Meir & Son, brown transfer, cup and saucer; a willow type tree is the focal point of the center pattern; small clusters of fruit trees and pagodas are scattered randomly on the white ground; cameos of a man fishing and large floral designs alternate on the border. $30.00 – 35.00.

"JOHN THOMSON" printed on a banner over a double circle with the pattern name "LAHORE" printed inside the top of the circle over the banner and "STONE CHINA" printed below the banner. This factory was located in Glasgow, Scotland, circa 1816 – 1884.

Plate 216. "Lahore," John Thomson, soup bowl, 10½"d; a man and woman are in the foreground; a large body of water separates the figures from a pagoda which has steps leading from its entrance to the water. $75.00 – 100.00.

Plate 217. "Net," Spode, circa 1810, dessert stand, 3½"h x 12"l, diamond-shaped, short pedestal base; reserves of pagodas and willow trees on a floral ground form a border on interior of dish. $400.00 – 500.00.

Plate 218. "Oriental," Ridgways, vegetable dish, 10½"l, footed, scalloped handles; the center pattern features three figures in the foreground with one standing and two seated on the ground beneath a large flowering tree; a large temple is across the river and other buildings are in the background; reserves of similar temple scenes alternate with floral reserves on the border. $125.00 – 150.00.

"RIDGWAYS" printed above an urn and beehive with the pattern name "ORIENTAL" printed in a bar below and the initials "W.R." printed below pattern name and "England," printed below initials, after 1891.

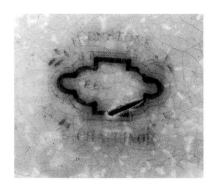

"E. Challinor" printed beneath a cartouche with "IRONSTONE" printed above, and the pattern name "PELEW" printed inside, circa 1842 – 1867.

Plate 219. "Pelew," E. Challinor, mulberry transfer, mitten relish; the scenic center pattern includes two temples connected by steps with an arched bridge in the background; flowers and trees complete the design; clusters of flowers are spaced around the inner border. $100.00 – 125.00.

Copeland mark on plate at right, initial "C" printed in a square with "COPELAND ENGLAND" below in green, circa after 1891, with an American retailer's mark of "Collamore & Co., New York City," printed in red.

Plate 220. "Queen Charlotte," Copeland, after 1891, plate, 9½"d. This pattern was originally made by Spode circa 1815 – 1820. The pattern has elements of a Willow pattern, but no willow tree! A teahouse, a bridge with two figures, and orange trees compose the center design with a Butterfly border pattern. **$60.00 – 75.00.**

Plate 221. "Siam," unmarked except for an 1850 registry mark, attributed to J. Clementson, sauce dish, 5"d, paneled shape; a large tree on a small hill and a curving path are in the foreground of the center pattern; a city with temples and minarets on either side of a river are in the background; smaller similar scenic reserves are in four spaces around the border on a wavy line diaper pattern. **$14.00 – 18.00.**

"T. Goodfellow" printed on a flowing banner of the garter mark, which has "IRONSTONE" printed at the top and the pattern name "SINGAN," printed inside, circa 1828 – 1859.

Plate 222. "Singan," T. Goodfellow, mulberry transfer, plate, 10"d, paneled shape; two men fishing from an arched bridge, a large willow tree, and small pagodas are the primary components of this scenic design highlighted by a floral border pattern. **$100.00 – 125.00.**

Plate 223. "The Temple," Podmore, Walker & Co., mulberry transfer, circa 1834 – 1859, handleless cup; a temple with a figure with a parasol and another temple are on either side of a large urn; a boat, trees, and other buildings are in the background; a scrolled design decorates the interior border of the cup. **$75.00 – 100.00.**

The following nine pictures are examples of the "Willow" pattern. There are several versions of Willow patterns. The most frequently seen is called the Traditional pattern. This design incorporates a tea house, a willow tree, a bridge with three figures, and two birds in flight. It is also distinguished by a border design based on one by Spode which is composed of wheels or circular shapes. The second most popular Willow pattern is known as "Two Temples II," which features two overlapping temples, two figures on a bridge, and one figure in the temple doorway. There are no birds in this pattern. A Butterfly border accompanies this pattern with butterfly shapes easily visible. The Two Temples II pattern is the same as Spode's "Broseley" pattern. Other factories, however, made the same design, and thus, unless marked with a Spode mark, examples are not attributed to Spode. There are several other variations which are described and illustrated in my book, Blue Willow, Revised Second Edition. Note that many Oriental landscape patterns are called Willow, even though one or more of the primary components of the Willow pattern are not part of the design.

Plate 224. "Willow" Traditional pattern, plate, 10"d, very soft glaze; unmarked, circa 1800. **$150.00 – 200.00.**

Plate 225. "Willow" Traditional pattern, sauce tureen with unique underplate with raised pedestal; unmarked, circa mid 1800s. **$500.00 – 600.00.**

Plate 226. "Willow" Traditional pattern, without a border, brown transfer, bone china, demitasse cup and saucer in octagonal shape highlighted with 22K gold bands; Wedgwood printed Portland Vase mark in blue on cup, circa 1879 – 1898. **$115.00 – 135.00.**

Plate 227. "Willow" Two Temples II pattern; the center design is heavily overlaid with gold scroll work: left: Tea bowl and saucer, porcelain; right: Coffee can and saucer, porcelain; attributed to New Hall Porcelain Works, circa 1795. **$225.00 – 250.00 each.**

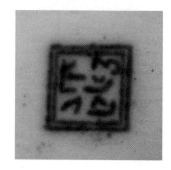

Miles Mason's Chinese characters printed mark in blue, circa 1800 – 1816.

Plate 228. "Willow" Two Temples II pattern, Miles Mason, cup and saucer. **$225.00 – 275.00.**

Plate 229. "Willow" Two Temples II pattern, bowl, 8½"d, gold rim, unmarked, circa 1800. **$125.00 – 150.00.**

Plate 230. "Willow" Two Temples II pattern in light blue, commemorative pitcher with "Joshua & Betty Roberts, 1833" printed in black over spout; unmarked, circa 1833. **$450.00 – 500.00.**

Charles James Mason's printed crown and drape mark in blue, circa 1845.

Plate 231. "Willow" pattern variation, Charles James Mason, sauce boat, 5½"l. This rendition of the pattern has a tea house and willow tree with a scroll work border. **$175.00 – 225.00.**

Plate 232. Willow variant pattern, unmarked, circa early 1800s, reticulated platter, 8¼" x 7¼"; dark cobalt blue transfer with a tea house and willow tree. **$250.00 – 350.00.**

Plate 233. Willow variant pattern, Spode, circa early 1800s, chestnut bowl; a tea house and two men on a bridge are the major components of this pattern. **$500.00 – 600.00.**

Ridgways printed bow and quiver mark in red with the pattern name "YEDDO" printed above a registry mark with the letter "D," denoting the year 1878.

Plate 234. "Yeddo," Ridgways, red transfer; the pattern featured two Oriental children at play with a scenic background; pitcher. **$125.00 – 150.00.**

The following eight pictures are of unidentified Oriental patterns made by different factories. Undoubtedly, these transfers had names, and perhaps they will surface at a later time.

Plate 235. Soup bowl decorated with a rare split transfer of two different scenes. A woman with a basket, a child, and a vase compose one scene. A sampan with one figure standing holding a fish and another seated under a canopy are the primary features of a figural water scene. This piece is attributed to Caughley, circa 1780. **$300.00 – 350.00.**

Plate 236. Plate, 9¾"d; three figures are on a pier: one is seated, one holds a cane, and one is gesturing toward a boat on the water; a large floral border surrounds the center pattern; Davenport printed mark in blue, circa 1805 – 1820. **$125.00 – 150.00.**

Grainger & Co. printed shield mark in blue with the initials "G. & Co. W," circa 1870 – 1889.

Plate 237. Sauce tureen and underplate, 7½"l x 6"h; Oriental landscape pattern with a temple decorates top of lid; a diaper design of flowers and geometric shapes forms a wide border on lid, top of bowl, and underplate; gold trim enhances rims, handles, and finials; Grainger & Co. **$275.00 – 325.00.**

Powell, Bishop & Stonier printed mark in green of a seated Oriental figure holding a parasol with "ORIENTAL" and "IVORY" printed on it, circa 1880.

Plate 238. Plate, 10½"d, two handles; green transfer pattern composed of a fan, a floral branch, a floral reserve, and two Chinese symbols; Powell, Bishop & Stonier. The mark on this plate contains the words "Oriental Ivory," but neither word is the pattern name because other patterns are found with the same mark. "Oriental" probably refers to the type of pattern, and "Ivory" to the color of the body glaze. $50.00 – 65.00.

Plate 239. Plate, 10"d, unmarked, circa mid 1800s; a fountain on the left, a large temple in the background, and a small figure in the foreground compose the primary elements of this Oriental landscape pattern. The transfer is a very dark blue accented by a very light blue inner border pattern. $225.00 – 250.00.

Plate 240. Tureen, ladle, and underplate; a pagoda, a bridge, and an island can be seen on the body of the tureen; a large floral design in the foreground also decorates the lid and the border of the underplate; the cobalt blue of this transfer flows, thus the pattern would be considered an example of Flow Blue; unmarked. $2,800.00 – 3,200.00 set.

Plate 241. Biscuit jar (without lid), 7"h, unmarked, circa mid 1800s; a series of temples and a long bridge with two figures compose the pattern along with large flowers and a flowering branch. This is not a "Willow" pattern, however, although one might think so at first glance. Unmarked, circa mid 1800s. **$175.00 – 225.00.**

Plate 242. Plate, 7"d, unmarked, circa mid 1800s, mulberry transfer; scenic and floral pattern featuring a mosque-type building and bridge in the center with figures in a small boat in the foreground. **$50.00 – 60.00.**

Chapter Five

 # Other Decorative Themes and Patterns

Although Oriental themes, in either monochrome or polychrome colors, are probably the most popularly collected type of English transfer decoration, other decorative themes were also widely produced. Historical subjects were very popular. Most importantly, for American collectors, however, several English manufacturers catered especially to the American market by printing patterns which incorporated American historical figures, events, and places. China was also decorated with English views and commemorative figures and events. Non-historical themes included portraits of popular figures of the day, figures from literature, and scenes featuring figures, couples, or groups, in Victorian dress, placed in pastoral or bucolic settings. Those types of figural scenes are collected today under the title of "Romantic Staffordshire." Additional non-Oriental scenic transfer designs included locations in other western European countries, landscapes, and nautical views to name a few. Animal and insect designs as well as floral and fruit patterns also were common.

Most of these non-Oriental transfer patterns are readily available on the secondary market, and most cost considerably less than the Oriental themes. There are, of course, exceptions, such as American historical views which can realize prices of several thousand dollars for some examples. Generally scenic views are higher in price than floral patterns. An exception would be the "Chintz" polychrome floral designs which were popular during the 1920s to 1930s. These have sparked collector interest over the last several years. Although they are twentieth century examples, a few patterns by several manufacturers have been included. The majority of examples in this chapter are monochrome patterns, but a number of colors other than blue are represented. Polychrome examples shown are basically floral in nature with the exception of a few examples of Prattware.

There are several general points to note regarding transfer patterns. The names of the patterns do not always reflect the design. Sometimes the same pattern name was used by different factories for different patterns. Distinctive border patterns, usually ornate in design, combining flowers, leaves, shells, and scroll work, as well as reserves complementing the center pattern, were used to accent the center pattern. Some border patterns were used by only one factory and thus can be used to identify the manufacturer when there is no factory mark on the piece. The same patterns could be and were used for many years in some cases. When one factory took over another, the back-mark might change, but the pattern would remain the same. Unfortunately some patterns are not marked with pattern names, although pattern names were routinely in use by the 1820s.

In this chapter, the transfer patterns are grouped into three categories: Animal, Bird, and Insect; Figural and Scenic; and Floral and Fruit. Historical figures and scenes are included within the Figural and Scenic category. In general, the pictures are arranged within each category by pattern name in alphabetical order. These are followed by unidentified patterns of the same genre but with identified factory marks. Last are examples without either a pattern name or a factory mark. The examples represent china made by numerous English factories, chiefly during the nineteenth century.

Animal, Bird, and Insect Themes

K. & Co. mark with pattern name, circa late 1800s.

Plate 243. Asiatic Pheasants, open vegetable bowl, 10½"l, light blue transfer. This was a popular pattern name used by several manufacturers for the same pattern or one similar to it. This example is marked "K. & Co.," which could be one of several factories, but is probably Keeling & Co. $150.00 – 200.00.

Plate 244. Devonshire, pattern name used for a series of bird patterns made by Ridgways from 1880. These have a registry mark for 1884. These scenic designs feature a different bird or game bird in one to three reserves on each piece. The examples shown here are in brown. Plate, 8¼"d, small birds in trees. $50.00 – 60.00.

Plate 245. Sauce dish, 4¾"d, heron by marsh. $20.00 – 25.00.

Plate 246. Plate, 9¼"d, a rooster at sunrise, a small bird in a tree, and fish underwater make up this design. $50.00 – 60.00.

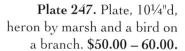

Plate 247. Plate, 10¼"d, heron by marsh and a bird on a branch. $50.00 – 60.00.

Plate 248. Fallow Deer, plate, 9"d, dark blue transfer, no manufacturer mark, circa 1830. This is not the same pattern which was made by John Rogers during a similar time period or by Wedgwood in the late 1880s. $175.00 – 200.00.

Plate 249. Godspeed the Plough, two-handled mug or loving cup imprinted on back and front with an ode to the farmer and farm animals, black transfer, unmarked, circa mid 1800s. $325.00 – 350.00.

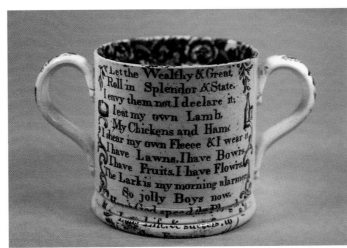

Ode on reverse of preceding cup.

Plate 250. Piping Shepherd, soup plate, 9½"d, unmarked, circa 1830, dark blue transfer. A woman sits under a tree with the shepherd standing and playing a musical instrument amid a flock of sheep. $250.00 – 275.00.

Plate 251. Pileated Woodpecker, plate, 10¾"d, a hand-colored transfer based on the original paintings by John J. Audubon. These were made as a series of plates by Adams after 1896. **$40.00 – 45.00.**

W. Adams & Sons mark on preceding plate.

Plate 252. Quadrupeds, berry bowl, 4"h, 5½"d, unmarked, circa 1820. A llama is the animal featured in this dark blue transfer. There are other quadruped patterns made by John Hall (see Williams, 1978, pgs. 660, 661) which are different from this example. **$325.00 – 350.00.**

"Rajah" printed pattern name on plate at right.

Plate 253. Rajah, plate, 10½"d, brown transfer pattern of elephants and an elaborate carriage in the center, elephant scenes are also in reserves around the border; unmarked, except for pattern name, circa mid to late 1800s. **$100.00 – 125.00.**

J.F. Wileman mark on plaque, circa 1869 – 1892.

Plate 254. Sporting Scene, octagon-shaped plaque, light blue transfer of hunting dogs, J.F. Wileman. **$150.00 – 175.00.**

Plate 255. Stag, saucer, 4½"d, dark pink transfer with a stag featured in the center reserve, unmarked except for the pattern name in a red garter mark and "750," circa mid 1800s. **$25.00 – 35.00.**

Powell, Bishop & Stonier mark with pattern name on soup plate, circa 1879 – 1891.

Plate 256. Wild Rose, soup plate, 10"d, brown transfer floral and bird design, Powell, Bishop & Stonier. **$35.00 – 40.00.**

Mark on Zoological Sketches (J.M. & L. or J.M. & S.), circa 1840s.

Plate 257. Zoological Sketches, animal and bird transfer in black, initials in mark are not fully legible, plate, 8"d. **$225.00 – 250.00.**

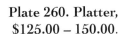

Unidentified Patterns with Manufacturers' Marks

Worcester mark on tea bowl at right. The impressed initials "B.F.B." with a crown was a mark used during the Barr, Flight & Barr period, circa 1807 – 1813.

Plate 258. Tea bowl, sepia transfer of insects, gold trim, Worcester. **$275.00 – 325.00.**

Plate 259. Game bird series, Brown-Westhead Moore & Co.; impressed company name mark with a registry mark for 1887, blue transfer. More examples in this series are shown in the next four photos. **Relish dish, $40.00 – 50.00.**

Plate 260. Platter, $125.00 – 150.00.

Plate 261. Plate, $40.00 – 50.00.

Plate 262. Covered vegetable, $100.00 – 125.00.

Plate 263. Plate, $40.00 – 50.00.

A. Bullock & Co. mark on tile, circa 1895 – 1915.

Plate 264. Tile, 6"d, brown transfer of a bird returning to it nest, A. Bullock & Co. **$65.00 – 75.00.**

Plate 265. Plate, 9½"d, brown transfer pattern of a butterfly and flowers, J. Dimmock & Co. mark with "Cliff" impressed, reflecting the name of the successor to the company (see Godden Mark 1291); an impressed date cypher indicates May 1885. **$30.00 – 40.00.**

Copeland printed mark on cup at right, after 1891.

Plate 266. Mush cup, black transfer of a hunter with his dogs, Copeland. **$125.00 – 150.00.**

Plate 267. Plate, 8¼"d, slate transfer of small birds and flowers, Ridgway, Sparks & Ridgway printed mark with a registry mark for 1877. **$25.00 – 35.00.**

Unidentified Patterns without Manufacturers' Marks

Plate 268. Cup and saucer, bird pattern, magenta transfer, unmarked, circa mid 1800s. **$100.00 – 120.00.**

Plate 269. Cup plate, 4¼"d, mulberry transfer of a dog frolicking, unmarked, circa 1840s. **$70.00 – 80.00.**

Plate 270. Cup and saucer, a young girl is feeding a sheep from a bowl, dark pink transfer, pink lustre trim, unmarked, circa 1850. **$125.00 – 150.00.**

Plate 271. Cup and saucer, black bat transfer (an early transfer technique), farm animals, unmarked, circa early 1800s. **$125.00 – 150.00.**

Plate 272. Pitcher, black transfer of horses on front with a horse and rider on reverse (not shown), pink lustre trim, unmarked, circa 1850. **$500.00 – 600.00.**

Plate 273. Platter, 19" x 16", scenic design with cows in the foreground, green transfer, unmarked. **$700.00 – 800.00.**

Figural and Scenic Designs

Prattware

Plate 274. This and the following three photographs illustrate a type of transfer called "Prattware." William Pratt decorated china with underglaze polychromed patterns from about 1780 to 1799. These early designs were highlighted by wide borders finished with solid glazes in rich colors. Examples are usually unmarked, and similar decorations were made by other factories during the same period until the mid 1800s. (The other scenic patterns shown in this section are in various monochrome colors and are arranged first by pattern name in alphabetical order, followed by examples without pattern names.) Prattware plate, 5½"d, scene commemorating the Sebastopol siege. **$150.00 – 175.00.**

Plate 275. Prattware plates, 5½"d: left, figural scene of two boys and a dog; right, scenic décor of cattle and ruins, border finished with a glossy red glaze. **$80.00 – 100.00 each.**

Plate 276. Prattware plate, 8"d, scenic design of a waterfall and ruins. **$125.00 – 150.00.**

Plate 277. Prattware compote decorated with an "English Factory" scene. Greek figures form a pattern around the inner border on a dark blue-black ground, circa 1850. **$300.00 – 350.00.**

Figural Scenes and Scenic Patterns by Pattern Name

Plate 278. Abbey Ruins, open vegetable, 12" x 10", Thomas Mayer, see Godden Mark 2568, circa 1836 – 1838, pink transfer. **$350.00 – 400.00.**

Plate 279. American Marine, Ashworth, see Godden Mark 145, the pattern name is also printed with the mark, circa 1890s, blue transfer. Left to right, top row: **Plate $60.00 – 75.00; Soup bowl, $50.00 – 70.00; Serving bowl, $175.00 – 225.00; Jug, $225.00 – 275.00; octagon-shaped saucers, $40.00 – 50.00 each;** bottom row: **Tea pot, $400.00 – 500.00; Bowl, $50.00 – 70.00; octagon-shaped saucers, $40.00 – 50.00 each; rectangular Bowl, $225.00 – 250.00; Plate, $60.00 – 75.00.**

Mark on plate at right with pattern name.

Plate 280. Baltimore & Ohio Railroad, Inclined View, Enoch Wood & Sons, circa 1818 – 1846, plate, 9¼"d, dark blue transfer, an historical American view scene. **$700.00 – 800.00.**

Marshall mark on plate with pattern name, circa 1884 – 1897.

Plate 281. Bosphorus, black and white transfer scene made by John Marshall, the Bo'Ness Pottery in Bo'-Ness Scotland, soup bowl, 9"d. **$125.00 – 150.00.**

Plate 282. Boston Mail's Gentleman's Cabin, American scene, attributed to J. & T. Edwards, circa 1839 – 1841, light blue transfer, pitcher. **$350.00 – 400.00.**

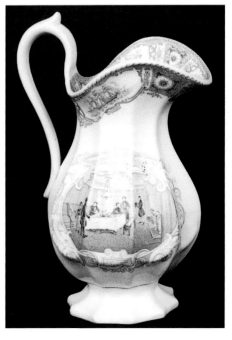

Plate 283. Boston State House (with **New York City Hall** on reverse), dark blue transfer, American views, attributed to Stubbs, circa 1822 – 1835, pitcher. **$1,200.00 – 1,400.00.**

F. Morley & Co. mark on plate, circa 1845 – 1858.

Plate 284. British Palaces (Buckingham Palace), English views, blue transfer, Francis Morley & Co., plate, **$400.00 – 450.00.**

Harding mark with pattern name, circa 1830 – 1840.

Plate 285. Canova, an urn, a gondola, and buildings compose this brown transfer scene. The mark appears to be W. & G. or W. & C. Harding. The pattern is similar to one by the same name made by Thomas Mayer and G. Phillips during the late 1820s to late 1840s, see Williams, 1978, p. 214. Platter, 12"d. **$300.00 – 350.00.**

Plate 286. Christmas Eve, dark blue transfer scene based on the art of Sir David Wilke, unmarked, attributed to Clews, circa 1818 – 1834, plate. **$250.00 – 300.00.**

Pattern name mark on handleless cup and saucer, circa 1845.

Plate 287. Cleopatra, a small urn with buildings in the background compose the center pattern, mulberry transfer with some hand-colored work, marked with pattern name only, handleless cup and saucer. **$75.00 – 100.00.**

Ralph Stevenson & Son mark with pattern name, circa 1832 – 1835.

Plate 288. Cologne, black scenic transfer featuring a river banked by mountains and a village, Ralph Stevenson & Son, plate, 10"d. **$200.00 – 250.00.**

Edge, Malkin & Co. mark, circa 1871 – 1899.

Plate 289. Como, Italy, sepia transfer, pastoral scene portraying a couple in a park setting with buildings in the background, Edge, Malkin & Co., large platter. **$400.00 – 500.00.**

Plate 290. Dr. Syntax Paints a Picture, dark blue transfer scene based on a print in a book by Rowlandson, Clews impressed mark, see Godden Mark, circa 1818 – 1834, plate, 10"d. **$300.00 – 350.00.**

Plate 291. Ealing Scene, English view of figures in boats in the foreground with a bridge and cottage in the background, sepia transfer, unmarked, circa 1830, plate, 9"d. **$120.00 – 140.00.**

Enoch Wood & Son mark on vegetable dish, circa 1818 – 1846.

Plate 292. English Cities, Salisbury, English views, light blue transfer, Enoch Wood & Son, open vegetable dish. $250.00 – 300.00.

Plate 293. English Views, English pastoral scene of a water wheel, river, and a village in the background, blue-green transfer, unmarked except for pattern name, plate, 10¼"d, circa mid 1800s. This is not the same pattern made by John Rogers between 1814 and 1836, see Williams, 1978, p. 256. $80.00 – 90.00.

Plate 294. Eton College, English view, brown transfer figural scene of a man, woman, and little girl dressed for a Sunday outing with a river and buildings in the background, unmarked, attributed to Edward & George Phillips, 1822 – 1834, see Godden Mark 3008 and Williams, 1978, p. 488; plate, 8¼"d. $150.00 – 200.00.

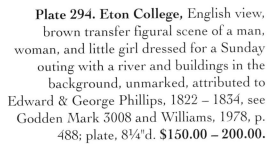

Plate 295. Foliage, mulberry transfer incorporating an urn and a large tree in the foreground with a bridge and towers in the background, unmarked, circa mid 1800s. This pattern by Walley is shown in Williams' *Flow Blue China and Mulberry Ware,* p. 157. Plate, 10¼"d, **$70.00 – 80.00.**

Pattern mark on small plate.

Plate 296. Fort Montgomery, Hudson River, black transfer, men on a log barge floating down the river, unmarked, circa early to mid 1800s, plate, 5"d. **$175.00 – 200.00 (mc).**

Clews printed pattern mark, "Genevese."

Plate 297. Genevese, Swiss scene, light blue transfer of a chalet and church, Clews impressed mark, see Godden Mark 919, circa 1818 – 1834, plate 10½"d. **$325.00 – 350.00.**

Enoch Wood &
Sons mark with pat-
tern name, circa
1818 – 1846.

Plate 298. Gondola, mulberry transfer, a large urn dominates
the center pattern with a river, gondola, and village in the background; gondolas are prominent in the three reserves around
the border, Enoch Wood & Sons, plate. **$150.00 – 175.00.**

Plate 299. Grecian Scenery, light blue
transfer, figures are in the foreground near a
ruin, a river and a gondola are in the background, unmarked except for pattern name,
circa 1860, plate, 9"d. **$70.00 – 80.00.**

Plate 300. Italian (Spode's Italian), blue
transfer, people and animals on a river
bank surrounded by a castle and other
buildings. This pattern was first introduced by the Spode company in 1816 and
still remains a popular pattern in current
production; this example is circa the mid
1800s. **$125.00 – 150.00.**

Plate 301. Ivanhoe, flow blue figural transfer scene titled "Rebecca Repelling the Templar." This scene is one in a series made by Wedgwood, circa 1899, plate, 10¼"d. $100.00 – 125.00.

Podmore, Walker & Co. mark on plate, circa 1834 – 1859.

Plate 302. Ivanhoe, light brown scenic transfer, a different pattern from the one in Plate 301; figures on a river bank are looking at a gazebo across the river, Podmore, Walker & Co., plate, $70.00 – 80.00.

Plate 303. Jenny Lind, light gray transfer with green, red, and yellow hand-colored accents, scenic view of figures in the foreground looking at a castle across the river with mountains in the background, Charles Meigh's impressed mark, see Godden Mark 2618, circa 1835 – 1849, large covered dish. $325.00 – 375.00.

Plate 304. Joseph's Travels Series, black transfers depict "Joseph's First Dream" and "Potiphar's Wife Falsely Accusing Joseph," unmarked, circa 1840, plates, 7"d. **$140.00 – 165.00 each.**

Thomas & Benjamin Godwin mark on soup bowl, circa 1809 – 1834.

Plate 305. Khanpore, India, scenic view of figures, river, and temples, gray-green transfer, Thomas & Benjamin Godwin, soup bowl. **$225.00 – 250.00.**

Pattern mark on plate, circa 1784 – 1790.

Plate 306. London View, The Lake Regent's Park, English view, a dark blue transfer scene, impressed name "Wood," (attributed to Enoch Wood 1784 – 1790) with printed pattern name, plate, 9¼"d. **$600.00 – 700.00.**

Plate 307. Lucano, dark blue scenic transfer of a tower and an arched bridge with cows in the foreground, Spode, circa 1810 – 1815, see Godden Mark 3651. Wash bowl, 13½"d. **$1,000.00 – 1,200.00.**

J.W. Pankhurst & Co. mark on plate, circa 1850 – 1882.

Plate 308. Lucerne, Swiss scenic view of chalets, lake, and a castle, mulberry transfer, J.W. Pankhurst & Co., plate, 9½"d. **$70.00 – 80.00.**

Pattern mark on plate, circa mid-1800s.

Plate 309. Mausoleum, light blue transfer, people are in a boat on a lake with monuments and buildings in the background, unmarked except for pattern name, plate, 10½"d. **$100.00 – 125.00.**

Joseph Heath & Co. mark with
pattern name, circa 1828 – 1841.

Plate 310. Milanese Pavilions, figural scene of two
women and a man in the foreground, mulberry transfer, Joseph Heath & Co. A different scene is shown
for this pattern name by Williams, 1978, p. 337, but
the borders are the same. Plate, **$100.00 – 125.00.**

Plate 311. Mount Vernon,
American view, magenta
transfer with silver lustre trim,
unmarked, circa 1810, cup
and saucer. **$200.00 – 225.00.**

Plate 312. Neptune, dark
gray transfer of boats,
unmarked, but attributed to J.
& G. Alcock, circa 1839 –
1846, see Williams, p. 648, tea
pot. **$250.00 – 275.00.**

Podmore, Walker & Co. mark with pattern name, circa 1834 – 1849.

Plate 313. Nerva, classical figural scene, brown transfer, Podmore, Walker & Co., plate, 8"d. **$60.00 – 70.00.**

Plate 314. Parisian Chateau, pastoral scene with cows in the foreground and a chateau in the background, Ralph Hall printed mark, circa 1822 – 1841 and impressed "Hall" mark, platter, 15"l x 12¼"w. **$250.00 – 300.00.**

Pattern mark on plate, after 1891.

Plate 315. Pastoral, blue transfer of a country scene with sheep in the foreground, unmarked except for pattern name and "England," plate, 10"d. **$50.00 – 60.00.**

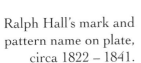

Ralph Hall's mark and pattern name on plate, circa 1822 – 1841.

Plate 316. Select Views, Pains Hill, Surrey, pastoral English scene, horses are in the foreground, and a manor house is in the background, dark blue transfer, Ralph Hall, plate, 10"d. **$250.00 – 275.00.**

W.H. Grindley & Co. mark with registry mark indicating a date of September, 1882.

Plate 317. Shakespeare, commemorative scene of the birthplace of William Shakespeare, brown transfer, W.H. Grindley & Co., plate, 8½"d. **$30.00 – 40.00.**

Pattern mark on plate, circa mid 1800s.

Plate 318. Sicilian, a brown scenic transfer incorporating flowers, a body of water, and an elaborately shaped structure, unmarked except for pattern name. See Williams, 1978, p. 416, for this same pattern with similar scenes. Plate, 8½"d. **$35.00 – 45.00.**

Plate 319. The Sower, figural scene of a farmer sowing seeds, red transfer, unmarked. The same transfer is shown by Williams, 1978, p. 526, with a wide floral border which carries a William Adams mark, circa 1800 – 1864. Handleless cup, 2½"h, 4"d. **$50.00 – 60.00.**

Pattern name on plate, circa after 1891.

Plate 320. Spanish Festivities, blue transfer of ladies in a coach with a monument in the background, unmarked except for pattern name and "England," plate, 9¼". **$90.00 – 100.00.**

Plate 321. Swiss, green transfer featuring a chalet, bridge, and body of water, Ralph Stevenson, sauce tureen and underplate. **$700.00 – 800.00.**

Ralph Stevenson mark and pattern name on sauce tureen and underplate, circa 1810 – 1832.

J. Clementson
mark on plate,
circa 1839 – 1864.

Plate 322. Sydenham, classical scene
dominated by a statue of a young
woman, brown transfer, J.
Clementson, plate, 8"d. **$45.00 – 60.00.**

Spode's impressed
mark on dessert dish.
This mark was in use
after 1784, see God-
den Mark 3648.

Plate 323. Tower (Spode's Tower), blue transfer of a tower and an arched bridge, impressed
Spode mark, circa 1820. Spode introduced this
pattern in 1815, and it is still produced today.
Dessert dish. **$400.00 – 450.00.**

Clementson mark
on pitcher with
pattern name, circa
1867 – 1880.

Plate 324. Udina, dark mulberry transfer, tall
buildings and a river with people in the foreground,
Clementson, pitcher, 5"h. **$75.00 – 100.00.**

Plate 325. **The Valentine,** dark blue figural scene based on the work of Sir David Wilke, unmarked, attributed to Clews, circa 1818 – 1834, plate. **$250.00 – 300.00.**

Plate 326. **Verona,** green transfer scene of a castle with a waterfall in the foreground, Charles Meigh's impressed mark, see Godden Mark 2618, circa 1849, plate, 6¾"d. **$40.00 – 50.00.**

Pattern name mark on plate, circa mid 1800s.

Plate 327. **Vignette,** black transfer figural scene, people are in the foreground and a large house is in the background, pink lustre border, unmarked except for pattern name, plate, 7"d. **$80.00 – 90.00.**

John Alcock
mark on plate,
circa 1853 – 1861.

Plate 328. Vincennes, mulberry
transfer, figural scene, John Alcock,
plate, 9½"d. **$100.00 – 125.00.**

Ashworth's mark
and pattern name
on tea tile, circa
1890 – 1900.

Plate 329. Vista (Mason's Vista), popular scenic
transfer which can be found in various colors. This
example was made by Ashworth, successor to Mason,
tea tile. **$115.00 – 125.00.**

Plate 330. Warwick Vase, brown
transfer, landscape scene incorporating a large vase or urn, Enoch Wood
& Sons, circa 1818 – 1846, platter,
15½"l x 13"w. **$250.00 – 300.00.**

Edward Walley mark on soup plate, circa 1845–1856.

Plate 331. Wild Rose, blue transfer, scene of people in boats, an arched bridge, and a large house, Edward Walley, soup plate, 9¼"d. **$150.00 – 175.00.**

Plate 332. Wild Rose, the same pattern as the preceding, shown here in brown, but this example is unmarked, platter, 18"l, circa mid-1800s. **$375.00 – 425.00.**

Unidentified Figural and Scenic Patterns with Manufacturers' Marks

Plate 333. Plate, 10"d, dark blue figural scene, three people are in the foreground and a large house and a castle are in the background, Clews, circa 1818 – 1834. **$150.00 – 200.00.**

Plate 334. Plate, 7¾"d, dark blue transfer, figural scene of a man fishing and two women reclining on the river bank; a large castle is in the background, Clews, circa 1818 – 1834. **$100.00 – 150.00.**

Clews impressed mark on plate, circa 1818 – 1834.

Plate 335. Plate, 9"d, dark blue transfer, figural river scene showing men fishing and people in a boat; two large domed buildings are in the background, Clews. **$150.00 – 200.00.**

Davenport impressed anchor mark, circa 1818.

Plate 336. Bowl, 12"l, rectangular shape, footed, light blue transfer, river scene with a large domed building in the background, Davenport. **$300.00 – 400.00.**

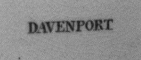

Davenport printed mark and impressed numbers (not visible) "10-67," circa 1867.

Plate 337. Soup plate, 9¼"d, light blue transfer scene of a river, buildings, and mountains, Davenport. **$175.00 – 195.00.**

Plate 338. Plate, 9¼"d, mulberry transfer of cows on a river bank with a large castle in the background, Scott Bros., Southwick Pottery, circa mid 1800s. **$100.00 – 125.00.**

Printed mark on soup bowl, initials "CEM" with "FLORENTINE CHINA," unidentified manufacturer, see Godden Marks 1101 and 1102 for Cork, Edge & Malkin, circa 1860 – 1871.

Plate 339. Soup bowl, 10½"d, light blue transfer, figures are in the boat, a cathedral-type building is in the background. The mark on this example is not identified. The mark could possibly be one for Cork, Edge & Malkin. **$150.00 – 175.00.**

Unidentified Figural and Scenic Patterns without Manufacturers' Marks

Plate 340. Pitcher, 6"h, mulberry transfer, figural scene, unmarked, circa 1840. **$350.00 – 375.00.**

Plate 341. Pitcher, 6"h, light blue transfer, figures on bank of river, unmarked, circa mid 1800s. **$115.00 – 125.00.**

Plate 342. Plate, 10"d, brown transfer, river scene with large buildings distinguished by several shapes of towers are on each bank, unmarked. **$100.00 – 125.00.**

Plate 343. Plate, 10"d, black transfer, a couple and a dog are shown in a park setting with large gothic buildings in the background, unmarked, circa mid-1800s. **$175.00 – 200.00.**

Plate 344. Vegetable dish with cover, six-sided, figural scene in a light blue transfer, circa mid-1800s, unmarked. **$250.00 – 300.00.**

Plate 345. Coffee cans and tray, black transfers; the figure of a young woman decorates the coffee can on the left; mythological figures are on the tray; and a farm scene is shown on the coffee can on the right, gilded trim, unmarked, circa 1815. **$300.00 – 400.00 set. (mc)**

Plate 346. Coffee pot, 11½"h, dark blue transfer, river scene featuring a figure in a boat with sail and people on the bank; buildings and mountains are in the background, unmarked, circa early 1800s. **$800.00 – 1,000.00.**

Floral and Fruit Designs by Pattern Name

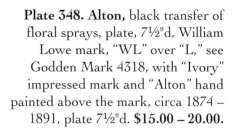

Henry Alcock printed mark, circa 1891 – 1910.

Plate 347. Alhambra, green transfer floral border pattern, Henry Alcock, plate, 10"d. **$50.00 – 75.00.**

Plate 348. Alton, black transfer of floral sprays, plate, 7½"d, William Lowe mark, "WL" over "L," see Godden Mark 4318, with "Ivory" impressed mark and "Alton" hand painted above the mark, circa 1874 – 1891, plate 7½"d. **$15.00 – 20.00.**

Plate 349. Arcadia, blue-green floral transfers scattered over bodies of pieces, Dunn Bennett & Co., circa 1875 – 1907. Wash bowl, pitcher, and small pitcher, **$275.00 – 325.00 set.**

Ridgway, Morley, Wear & Co. mark with pattern name, circa 1836 – 1842.

Plate 350. Caledonian, gray-green geometric and floral transfer, Ridgway, Morley, Wear & Co. Dinner plate, soup bowl, fruit bowl, and salad plate, **$100.00 – 125.00 set (mc).**

Plate 351. Chrysanthemum, light black floral transfer, John Edwards mark, see Godden Mark 1452, and a registry mark for 1893, bowl, 9"d. **$15.00 – 20.00.**

Plate 352. Cleveland, sepia floral pattern, Clementson Bros., printed Phoenix mark with "England," circa 1891 – 1910, plate, 9"d. **$20.00 – 25.00.**

Doulton printed mark with pattern name.

Plate 353. Elaine, brown transfer center pattern depicting an urn of flowers; Doulton mark with a registry number for 1887, plate, 9"d. **$25.00 – 30.00.**

G.L. Ashworth & Bros., printed and impressed marks, circa 1862 – 1890.

Plate 354. Empress, small floral medallion in center with a wide floral border, brown transfer, G.L. Ashworth & Bros., plate, 8"d. **$20.00 – 25.00.**

Plate 355. Essex, light black transfer of floral sprays on each side of piece, J. & G. Meakin, circa after 1890, plate, 8"d. **$20.00 – 25.00.**

Plate 356. Flower Cross, blue transfer pattern covering piece, unmarked, a rare pattern attributed to Spode, circa 1810, plate, 9¼"d. **$300.00 – 325.00.**

Printed pattern name on dessert dish, circa 1845.

Plate 357. Fruit Basket, polychrome fruit pattern, unmarked except for pattern name, possibly made by William Smith & Co., see Williams, 1978, p. 632; dessert dish, 11"l. **$125.00 – 145.00.**

Plate 358. Hythe, Art Nouveau floral pattern in blue, Keeling & Co., wash bowl and pitcher. **$800.00 – 1,000.00 set.**

Keeling & Co. mark on bowl and pitcher set and dresser set, circa 1912 – 1936.

Plate 359. Dresser set in the **Hythe** pattern, ten pieces: pair of candle holders, covered jar, covered soap dish, two small vases, hair receiver, ring tree, two covered powder jars and tray. **$800.00 – 1,000.00 set.**

Plate 360. Iris, blue Art Nouveau floral pattern, A.J. Wilkinson, Royal Staffordshire Pottery, see Godden Mark 4170, circa 1907. **$250.00 – 300.00.**

Plate 361. Lace, sepia transfer, the floral medallion in the center is repeated in the border design, Johnson Bros., circa 1891 – 1913, plate, 9"d. **$15.00 – 20.00.**

Davenport printed mark on plate, circa 1820 – 1860.

Plate 362. Lilium, a polychrome floral pattern on a deep rose ground covers surface except for a small undecorated center circle, Davenport, plate, 9½"d. **$140.00 – 165.00.**

Plate 363. **Meissen,** blue floral transfer design, Brown-Westhead, Moore & Co., see Godden Mark 684, circa 1895 – 1904, plate, 9"d. **$25.00 – 30.00.**

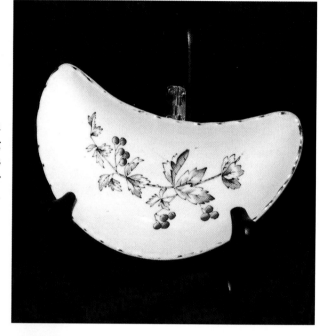

Plate 364. **Minerva,** brown floral and fruit pattern is highlighted with light orange, see following example for the complete pattern; John Edwards garter-style printed mark with a registry number for 1889, bone dish, 6¼"d. **$15.00 – 20.00.**

Plate 365. **Minerva,** full pattern, accented with light orange and blue, John Edwards mark with a registration number for body design for 1888 and a registration number for pattern for 1889, platter, 12" x 9". **$100.00 – 125.00.**

Plate 366. Moss Rose, floral transfer with hand-colored accents, attributed to Whittingham, Ford & Co., circa 1868 – 1873. The mark is composed of the royal arms and a banner with the initials "W-F," and "Ironstone China" printed below, toothbrush holder, 5"h. **$60.00 – 75.00.**

Baker & Co. mark with pattern name, circa 1860 – 1893.

Plate 367. Persian Rose, brown floral transfer, Baker & Co., Plate, 9"d. **$20.00 – 25.00.**

Plate 368. Queen Charlotte, pearl ware body, slate blue floral transfer; a floral medallion composes the center pattern; reserves of urns or bowls, flanked by "grotesques," (Wedgwood term for dragon designs) form the border design, Wedgwood, circa 1885. **$85.00 – 95.00.**

Plate 369. Raleigh, Art Nouveau floral pattern shown in blue and white and flow blue, Burgess & Leigh printed mark with a registry mark for 1902. Left, covered vegetable bowl, blue transfer, **$175.00 – 225.00;** right, covered vegetable bowl, flow blue transfer, **$300.00 – 400.00.**

T.G. & F. Booth mark on butter pat, circa 1883 – 1891.

Plate 370. Rosaline, brown floral pattern, T.G. & F. Booth, butter pat, 2"d. **$15.00 – 20.00.**

Plate 371. Rose, mulberry floral transfer, unmarked but the pattern is the same as one by Edward Challinor, see Williams, *Flow Blue China and Mulberry Ware,* p. 179, circa 1862, plate, 10"d. **$75.00 – 85.00.**

Holmes, Plant & Maydew printed mark with a registry mark for 1882.

Plate 372. Seine, black floral transfer, Holmes, Plant & Maydew, cup and saucer. **$35.00 – 40.00.**

Brown-Westhead Moore & Co., printed mark, circa after 1862.

Plate 373. Teutonic, blue floral transfer covers surface of plate, geometric border design, Brown-Westhead Moore & Co., plate, 10"d. **$100.00 – 125.00.**

Plate 374. Utopia, sepia floral transfer around top third of piece, Henry Alcock, circa 1891 – 1900, pitcher, 8"h. **$60.00 – 75.00.**

Plate 375. Ventnor, light brown floral transfer accented with yellow, pink, and blue, Sampson Hancock & Sons, circa 1906 – 1912, see Godden Mark 1932, plate, 9". **$15.00 – 20.00.**

Pattern mark on toothbrush holder, circa mid 1800s.

Plate 376. Vesta, brown transfer floral border pattern, unmarked except for pattern name, toothbrush holder. **$150.00 – 175.00.**

Plate 377. Wall Flower, gray transfer floral pattern with red-orange enamel accenting flowers, John Edwards, circa 1880 – 1900, see Godden Mark 1452, plate, 8"d. **$20.00 – 25.00.**

Unidentified Floral and Fruit Patterns with Manufacturers' Marks

Plate 378. Cup plate, 4"d, dark brown transfer. The pattern is primarily floral except for the cameo of a person at the top and the monogram "MMR." The piece carries the impressed mark, "ADAMS," circa 1800 – 1864. **$40.00 – 50.00.**

Plate 379. Nut dish, 4½" sq., brown transfer floral spray with red and yellow accents, Henry Alcock, Godden Mark 65, circa 1891 – 1910. **$10.00 – 15.00.**

Plate 380. Bowl, 7¼" sq., wide border pattern incorporating floral designs, brown transfer, T. & R. Boote, Ltd. The mark is similar to Godden Mark 439 and has a registry pattern mark for 1886 and a body registration mark for 1884. **$20.00 – 25.00.**

Plate 381. Plate, 7¼" sq., folded edges, floral and fruit pattern; dark brown coloring on leaves with berries and stems painted blue, matching the glaze on the corners of dish, Sampson Bridgwood & Son, Godden Mark 595, circa 1885. **$50.00 – 60.00.**

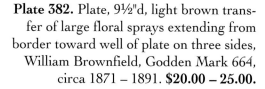

Plate 382. Plate, 9½"d, light brown transfer of large floral sprays extending from border toward well of plate on three sides, William Brownfield, Godden Mark 664, circa 1871 – 1891. **$20.00 – 25.00.**

Plate 383. Platter, 12" x 9½", polychrome floral pattern in rust-brown, yellow, and green. Brownfield Guild Pottery, Godden Mark 668, circa 1891 – 1898. **$75.00 – 100.00.**

Plate 384. Platter, 10" x 7½"; brown floral transfer border pattern with light touches of yellow and green on some flowers, two Clementson Bros. marks, see Godden Marks 906 and 907; there is also a number indicating the design was registered in 1894. **$50.00 – 75.00.**

Plate 385. Platter, 6" x 8¾"; slate blue floral transfer border pattern composed of scrollwork framing each flower, John Maddock mark, see Godden Mark, 2462, circa 1880 – 1896. **$20.00 – 25.00.**

Plate 386. Plate, 9¾"d, a light brown floral design around the border is highlighted with light blue, pink, and yellow; A. Meakin, the mark is similar to Godden Mark 2586, circa 1891 – 1897. **$15.00 – 20.00.**

Plate 387. Plate, 9¾"d, gray transfer pattern of a large floral spray on one side of plate and a smaller one on the other side, accented with a bright yellow, orange, and blue, Powell & Bishop, see Godden Mark 3136, circa 1876 – 1878. **$20.00 – 25.00.**

Plate 388. Plate, 9½"d, dark slate floral pattern decorates bottom half of plate, G.W. Turner & Sons, Godden Mark 3895, circa 1891 – 1895. **$20.00 – 25.00.**

Plate 389. Plate, 9"d, polychrome floral pattern in orange, yellow, and lavender, Upper Hanley Pottery, Godden Mark 3928, circa 1895 – 1900. **$25.00 – 30.00.**

Plate 390. Plate, 8½"d, magenta floral transfers decorate each of six lightly molded sections of the plate on a pale yellow ground, Worcester, Godden Mark 4350 with year cypher for 1889, and "Tice & Huntington, Cincinnati" importing mark. **$40.00 – 50.00.**

Unidentified Floral Patterns without Manufacturers' Marks

Plate 391. Meat drainer, 13½"l, brown transfer border pattern incorporating shells, beads, and flowers, unmarked, circa mid 1800s. **$200.00 – 225.00.**

Plate 392. Mug, 4"h, lavender floral transfer, unmarked, circa 1820. **$85.00 – 95.00.**

Plate 393. Handleless cup and cup plate, polychrome fruit and floral transfer, unmarked, circa mid 1800s. **$70.00 – 80.00 set.**

Chintz Patterns

The last group of floral transfer patterns represents "chintz" designs which were made by a number of English factories from the early 1900s. Examples popular today, though, were made by several companies primarily during the 1930s and 1940s. A few of these patterns are included here because of their current popularity. There are several references, however, devoted solely to this type of decoration. "Chintz" refers to a polychrome floral transfer pattern which covers the entire surface of a piece of china without a separate border pattern. This form of ceramic decoration became very collectible on the American market during the 1990s. For pieces which originally sold for very little, hundreds of dollars are now paid. The pieces usually have pattern names and are also identified by various names associated with the factory marks, such as "Royal Winton" (used in marks by Grimwades), "Lord Nelson," (used by Elijah Cotton), and "Crown Ducal" (used by A.G. Richardson & Co.) Collectors should be aware that reproductions of chintz patterns are now being offered by wholesale companies which market reproductions to the antique trade.

Plate 394. Crown Ducal, **Ivory Fruit** pattern, biscuit barrel. **$200.00 – 225.00.**

Plate 395. Crown Ducal, **Blue Chintz,** covered butter dish. **$200.00 – 250.00.**

Plate 396. James Kent, **Hydrangea** pattern, plate, 6"d. **$65.00 – 75.00.**

167

Plate 397. Lord Nelson, **Briar Rose** pattern, tray. $125.00 – 150.00.

Plate 398. Royal Winton, **Balmoral** pattern, candy dish. $650.00 – 700.00.

Plate 399. Royal Winton, **Julia** pattern, tray. $350.00 – 400.00.

Plate 400. Shelly Potteries, Ltd., **Melody** pattern, biscuit barrel. $575.00 – 625.00.

Chapter Six

Novelty China

English china is basically thought of in terms of table wares and art objects, but another facet of the industry focuses on some novelties made for amusement as well as decoration. One category of novelties is Staffordshire figures. The ceramic figures were made in the likeness of people, animals, or buildings. Most represent a form of folk art. They were made of simple earthenware, and features were generally not fashioned with great detail. Pieces were usually colorfully painted, some under the glaze and others over the glaze. They were mass produced and sold as inexpensive china to decorate the mantels of cottages of the working classes. Some were made in the image of famous people of the era. These types of figures have been made since the 1700s, and they continue to be made today. Most examples were unmarked, and because they were made by various potters in the Staffordshire district, the name "Staffordshire Figures" evolved to identify that type of production. Those figures made prior to the mid 1800s are full, rounded figures while those produced after that time were usually made with a flat back (Pozo, p. 15).

Early Staffordshire figures bring large prices. Those sold at recent auctions have realized much greater prices than the pre-sale estimates. Consequently, a reproduction market is active today for these figures, especially the animals. Wholesale catalogs advertise a variety of figures which are sold to antique and collectible outlets. Collectors should examine pieces carefully for signs of age and also be wary of prices which are usually much less expensive. A large display of such figures by a retail outlet also is a clue that the figures are probably not too old.

A number of Staffordshire figures are illustrated in this chapter as well as some other china novelties such as a Nesting Hen, Cow Creamers, Toby Jugs, and Sugar Dusters which are similar in nature to the figures. Most of the examples are unmarked but basically date from the mid to late Victorian era, with a few exceptions representing eighteenth century pieces.

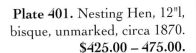

Plate 401. Nesting Hen, 12"l, bisque, unmarked, circa 1870. $425.00 – 475.00.

Plate 402. Cow creamers, 5"l, examples of "Redware" or "Jackfield ware," identified by a red clay body covered with a glossy black glaze, circa 1860. **$275.00 – 325.00 each.**

Plate 403. Sugar duster, 6"h, beige and dark brown colors. Rotund figures painted in bright colors with perforations in their hats were popular as sugar shakers in Victorian times; unmarked, circa 1870. These were also called "Prestopans" because they originated from potteries in Prestopan, Scotland, during the early 1800s. Not only were sugar dusters made in this figural form, but also similar figures were made for other spices and condiments such as pepper, mustard, and vinegar. **$400.00 – 450.00.**

Plate 404. Sugar duster, 5"h, cobalt blue and red colors, unmarked, circa 1870. **$400.00 – 450.00.**

Plate 405. Toby jug, 11"h, undecorated white ware, made in the image of John Bull, a name coined to represent the common Englishman, unmarked, circa late 1700s. Toby jugs were made for drinking or pouring ale. They are characterized by a pot-bellied figure, usually holding a mug of beer and wearing a tri-cornered hat. The origin of the Toby is not known, although Lewis (p. 93) notes that it may have been based on "a literary figure of 'Uncle Toby,' or a popular song, 'The Little Brown Jug,' dedicated to Toby Philpot and written in 1761." Lewis also notes that the first documented Toby was one dated 1785. **$550.00 – 650.00 (mc).**

Plate 406. Toby jug, 9½"h, unmarked, Whieldon type glaze, a brown mottled underglaze decoration used by Thomas Whieldon in the mid to late eighteenth century. **$500.00 – 600.00.**

Plate 407. Toby, 8½"h, seated figure holding a mug of ale, unmarked, circa 1880. **$400.00 – 500.00.**

Plate 408. Toby, 6"h, a "Merry Christmas" version decorated with holly, unmarked, late Victorian. $400.00 – 500.00.

Plate 409. Candle snuffer, 3"h, figure in colorful dress with a black tri-cornered hat, unmarked, attributed to Minton, circa 1795. $1,000.00 – 1,100.00.

Derby hand-painted mark on figure; initials "S" and "H" refer to the owners of the company at the time, Stevenson & Hancock, see Godden Marks 1267 and p. 597.

Plate 410. Figure, 4½"h, representing "Dr. Syntax," Derby factory, after 1861. $850.00 – 950.00.

Plate 411. Staffordshire figure, King John Signing the Magna Carta, 12½"h, unmarked, circa mid 1800s. **$1,500.00 – 1,800.00.**

Plate 412. Highlander and sheep figure, 11¾"h, unmarked, circa mid 1800s. **$700.00 – 800.00.**

Plate 413. Highlander and dog figure, 12"h, unmarked, circa mid 1800s. **$800.00 – 900.00.**

Plate 414. Red Riding Hood figure, unmarked, circa mid 1800s. **$500.00 – 600.00.**

Plate 415. Highland Girl, 13"h, unpainted, unmarked, circa mid 1800s. **$600.00 – 700.00.**

Plate 416. Spaniel, 16"h, Staffordshire "Redware" or "Jackfield" ware, glossy black glaze over a red clay body, unmarked, circa 1800. **$475.00 – 575.00.**

Plate 417. Spaniel, 10½"h, only nose, eyes, and paws painted, unmarked, circa mid 1800s. **$300.00 – 400.00.**

Plate 418. Spaniels, black and white, 9½"h, unmarked, circa 1870. **$800.00 – 900.00 pair.**

Plate 419. Whippets, unmarked, circa 1870. **$1,200.00 – 1,400.00 pair.**

Plate 420. Cottage pocket watch holder, unmarked, circa 1860. **$600.00 – 700.00.**

Plate 421. Castle spill holder vase (to hold spills for lighting fires), 7½"h, unmarked, circa late 1800s. **$300.00 – 400.00.**

Chapter Seven

Royal Commemoratives

Royal Commemoratives are a specific category of collectible china, and numerous references are available on that subject. This last chapter on Royal Commemoratives has been included, however, to somewhat pull together the various types of decorations found on English china in general. Examples also exhibit many variations as to ceramic body types, decoration methods, and objects. Simple earthenwares, stonewares, and bone china can be found. Molded and applied designs as well as different glazes and transfer work were used for decoration. Objects range from bar measures and wine jugs to cups, mugs, plates, pitchers, and vases. The Royal Commemoratives also reflect a long historical period which consequently reflects the production history of the English pottery industry. Examples shown here are arranged by date or time period.

Plate 422. Bar measure, 9½"h, stoneware. The light gray body of the piece has been painted a dark cobalt blue, framing flowers and a split apple on either side of a lightly embossed crest with a crown. The initials "GR" are painted in cobalt blue on top of the crest. The piece is unmarked but is attributed as being made during the reign of George III who ruled from 1760 – 1820. Commemoratives from his reign are relatively rare. **$800.00 – 1,000.00.**

Plate 423. Plate, 6"d, earthenware with molded leaf design around border; brown transfer of King George III, a small boy, and a quotation, "I hope the time will come when every child in my dominion will be able to read the Bible." These plates are associated with Joseph Lancaster who, during the early 1800s, administered the Lancasterian schools for the children of the poor. The plate probably dates circa 1820, after the death of King George III. **$800.00 – 1,000.00.**

Plate 424. Mourning pitcher, 6½"h, for King George IV, earthenware, applied braided work on handle, black transfer portrait on front; Goodwin, Bridgwood & Harris, circa 1830. The mourning pitcher was also made with a brown transfer portrait. $800.00 – 1,000.00.

Reverse of mourning pitcher with an inscription, "TO THE MEMORY OF HIS LATE MAJESTY, KING GEORGE IV, Born Aug. 12, 1762, Ascended the Throne, January 29, 1820, Publicly Proclaimed (January) 31 (1820). Departed This Life June 26, 1830, Aged 68 Years."

Plate 425. Pitcher, 7"h, commemorating the reign of King William IV and Queen Adelaide from 1830 to 1837, soft paste, heavily embossed design on body, blue transfer portraits, unmarked, King William's portrait. $400.00 – 600.00.

Reverse of commemorative pitcher with Queen Adelaide's portrait.

Plate 426. Pitcher, 7¼"h, commemorating the coronation of King William IV and Queen Adelaide who were crowned on September 8, 1831, mulberry transfer with center inscription. $400.00 – 500.00.

One side of preceding pitcher with transfer portrait of King William IV.

Another side of pitcher with transfer portrait of Queen Adelaide.

Plate 427. Plate, 7¼"d, earthenware with molded floral border, green transfer portrait of Queen Victoria and inscription, "VICTORIA REGINA Born 25th of May 1819, Proclaimed 20th of June, 1837," a commemorative for Queen Victoria's ascension to the throne, unmarked. **$800.00 – 1,000.00.**

Plate 428. Square plate depicting Queen Victoria and Prince Albert, dark pink transfer figural portraits of the couple, "Victoria & Albert" printed beneath portrait, unmarked, circa 1850. **$600.00 – 700.00.**

Plate 429. Tea cup and tea bowl, decorated with the same portrait as the preceding plate, but Victoria's skirt is painted with a blue-green color, and there is a pink lustre finish around the interior border of the cup. **$400.00 – 500.00 each.**

Plate 430. Tea pot matching preceding pieces. $1,000.00 – 1,200.00.

Plate 431. Staffordshire pitcher, 6"h, with very ornate handle; pink transfer portraits of Queen Victoria, in her wedding attire, and Prince Albert; copper lustre finish on top, base, and handle; the panels framing the portraits are enameled in canary yellow, and some examples were also made with blue panels, unmarked, after 1840. **$500.00 – 600.00.**

Plate 432. Stoneware pitcher with busts in relief of Queen Victoria on one side and Prince Albert on the other, deep rust-brown glaze, unmarked, after 1840. **$400.00 – 500.00.**

Reverse of stoneware jug showing bust of Prince Albert.

Plate 433. Stoneware jug, 7½"h, dark brown glaze on top; relief figure of Queen Victoria, unmarked, after 1840. **$400.00 – 500.00.**

Reverse of jug showing figure of Prince Albert.

Impressed mark on mourning pitcher with registry mark for 1862.

Plate 434. Mourning pitcher, 7½"h, commemorating Prince Albert's death in 1861; stoneware with a pebbled surface; bust of Prince Albert in relief with "Prince Consort" inscribed beneath portrait on front side and "Born 1819 — Died 1861" inscribed on reverse; impressed initials "CHBOL" over a registry mark for the year 1862. Different sizes of these pitchers were made, and some have plated lids. **$600.00 – 700.00.**

Plate 435. Mug, 3½"h, black transfer portrait of Queen Victoria commemorating her Golden Jubilee year in 1887, unmarked. **$225.00 – 275.00.**

One side of mug with inscription, "Jubilee of Her Majesty Queen Victoria 1887."

Another side of mug showing Buckingham Palace.

Plate 436. Loving cup, 3 handles, 6½"h, stoneware, commemorating the silver anniversary of the Prince and Princess of Wales, Albert Edward and Alexandra, in 1888, Doulton. This side portrays Prince Albert Edward. **$300.00 – 400.00.**

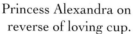

Princess Alexandra on reverse of loving cup.

Printed message on loving cup.

Aynsley mark on pitcher, noting that this example was No. 23 in a limited edition of 400; artist signature.

Plate 437. Pitcher, 8¼"h, bone china, portrait of Queen Victoria on front with "Souvenir of Her Majesty Queen Victoria" printed above portrait with the date "1837" on one side and "1897" on the other side; "Empress of India" is printed below portrait; a commemorative of Queen Victoria's Diamond Jubilee; Aynsley, limited edition of 400 with artist signature. $800.00 – 1,000.00.

Inscription on back of Diamond Jubilee beaker.

Plate 438. Beaker, 3¾"h, earthenware, brown transfer portrait of Queen Victoria, commemorating her Diamond Jubilee in 1897, Doulton. $300.00 – 400.00.

Mark on base of Diamond Jubilee beaker.

Plate 439. Pitcher, 8"h, brown transfer portrait, commemorating the long reign of Queen Victoria, 1837 – 1897, Diamond Jubilee item, Campbellfield Pottery Co., Glasgow, Scotland. **$400.00 – 500.00.**

Reverse of Diamond Jubilee pitcher, multicolored transfer of Balmoral, the royal residence in Scotland.

Campbellfield Pottery Co. mark on Diamond Jubilee pitcher.

Plate 440. Pitcher, 5"h, Diamond Jubilee commemorative for Queen Victoria, *pâte sur pâte* portrait on a dark green glazed ground, Copeland. **$200.00 – 300.00.**

Copeland printed mark on jubilee pitcher, circa 1892; year indicates pitcher was made several years prior to the jubilee year.

Plate 440a. Reverse of preceding pitcher with a *pâte sur pâte* shield inscribed with "Victoria Queen and Empress 1837," and below shield, "Diamond Jubilee, 1897," Copeland.

Plate 441. Queen Victoria Diamond Jubilee beaker, stoneware with a dark cobalt blue glaze; relief images of the Queen in 1837 and in 1897, Doulton. **$300.00 – 400.00.**

Plate 442. Edward VII Coronation commemorative beaker, 3½"h, earthenware, June 1902, Royal Doulton. **$175.00 – 225.00.**

Reverse of Edward VII beaker, with an inscription, "The King's Coronation Dinner, June 1902."

Plate 443. Edward VII Coronation commemorative cup, earthenware, inscribed "June 26th, 1902," multicolored transfers, marked "Foley China," (Robinson & Son). **$200.00 – 250.00.**

Plate 444. Pitcher, 7"h, earthenware with a dark brown glaze; multicolored transfer portraits of Queen Alexandra and King Edward VII, unmarked. **$300.00 – 400.00.**

Plate 445. Tea pot, earthenware with a dark brown glaze and decorated with the same transfers of Queen Alexandra and King Edward VII as the preceding pitcher, unmarked. **$400.00 – 500.00.**

Plate 446. Edward VII Coronation commemorative mug, green transfer portraits of the King and Queen, Royal Doulton. **$175.00 – 225.00.**

Inscription on back of mug, "Long Life And Happiness To King Edward VII And His Beloved Consort, Queen Alexandra Crowned June 16th 1902."

Plate 447. Edward VII Coronation commemorative beaker, 4"h, multicolored transfer portraits, with dates of marriage, 1893, and coronation, 1902, S. Fielding & Co. **$175.00 – 225.00.**

Reverse of preceding beaker with a banner inscribed with "May Your Reign Be Glorious."

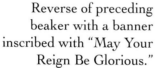

Plate 448. Memorial pitcher, 7¾"h, inscribed "Peace (King Edward VII) Maker Born Nov. 9th 1841 — Died May 6, 1910," unmarked. **$300.00 – 400.00.**

Plate 449. George V Coronation commemorative mug, 1911, multicolored transfer portraits of King George V and Queen Mary, Shelly China Co. **$150.00 – 200.00.**

Reverse of preceding mug printed with a coat of arms and "Urban District of Chadderton."

Plate 450. Coronation commemorative pitcher, 6½"h, olive green and cobalt blue majolica decorated with busts in relief of King George V and Queen Mary on either side, 1911, Doulton. Bust of George V. **$300.00 – 400.00.**

Bust of Queen Mary on reverse side of Doulton pitcher.

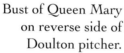

Inscription on center of pitcher, "The Coronation of King George V and Queen Mary."

Plate 451. Coronation commemorative plate with multicolored transfer portraits of King George V and Queen Mary and inscribed "May Their Reign Be Glorious," unmarked. $125.00 – 150.00.

Plate 452. Figural pitchers, 6"h, of King George V and Queen Mary, hand painted, unmarked. $100.00 – 125.00 each.

Plate 453. Vase or loving cup, 7½"h, Coronation commemorative with portraits of King George V and Queen Mary, inscribed with "Coronation 1911" and "Ascension 1910." Copeland mark with T. Goode & Co. retailer's mark. **$1,500.00 – 2,000.00.**

Reverse of vase with a list of Commonwealth countries.

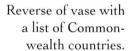

Mark on base, noting that a limited edition of 100 was made. This one is number 19; Copeland factory printed mark and T. Goode & Co. printed retailer's mark.

Plate 454. Whiskey or wine bottle, stoneware, 8"h, George V Coronation commemorative, June 22, 1911, *pâte sur pâte* portraits of the King and Queen on a dark green glazed ground, Copeland. **$400.00 – 500.00.**

Reverse of bottle with the name of the distillery in Edinburgh, Scotland.

Bibliography

Bagdade, Susan and Al. *Warman's English & Continental Pottery & Porcelain*. Willow Grove, PA: Warman Publishing Co., Inc., 1987.

___. *Warman's English & Continental Pottery & Porcelain, 3rd Edition*. Iola, WI: Krause Publishing, 1998.

Barber, Edwin Atlee. *The Ceramic Collector's Glossary*. New York: Da Capo Press, 1967 (first published in New York in 1914 by the Walpole Society).

Boger, Louise-Ade. *The Dictionary of World Pottery and Porcelain*. New York: Charles Scribner's Sons, 1971.

Burton, K.J. *Pottery in England From 3500 BC – AD 1950*. South Brunswick and New York: A.S. Barnes and Company, 1975.

Caiger-Smith, Alan. *Lustre Pottery*. London: Faber and Faber, 1985.

Camehl, Ada Walker. *The Blue-China Book*. New York: Dover Publications, Inc., 1971 (originally published 1916).

Cooper, Ronald G. *English Slipware Dishes 1650 – 1850*. New York: Transatlantic Arts, 1968.

Copeland, Robert. *Spode's Willow Pattern and Other Designs after the Chinese*. New York: Rizzoli, 1980

Coysh, A.W. *Blue and White Transfer Ware 1780 – 1840*. Rutland, Vermont: A.W. Coysh, 1971.

Gaston, Mary Frank. *Blue Willow, Second Edition*. Paducah, KY: Collector Books, 1990.

___. *Collector's Encyclopedia of Flow Blue China*. Paducah, KY: Collector Books, 1983.

___. *Collector's Encyclopedia of Limoges Porcelain*. Paducah, KY: Collector Books, 1980.

Godden, Geoffrey A. *British Pottery, An Illustrated Guide*. London: Barrie & Jenkins, 1974.

___. *Encyclopedia of British Pottery and Porcelain Marks*. New York: Crown Publishers, 1964.

___. *British Pottery and Porcelain 1780 – 1850*. New York: A.S. Barnes and Company, Inc., 1963.

___. *Victorian Porcelain*. New York: Thomas Nelson & Sons, 1961.

Husfloen, Kyle (ed). *Pottery and Porcelain Ceramic Price Guide, 2nd Edition*. Dubuque, IA: Antique Trader Books, 1997.

Huxford, Sharon and Bob (eds). *Schroeder's Antiques Price Guide, Nineteenth Edition*. Paducah, KY: Collector Books, 2001.

Griselda, Lewis. *A Collector's History of English Pottery, Fourth Revised Edition*. Woodbridge, Suffolk, England: Antique Collector's Club, Ltd., 1981; reprinted 1992 (first published in 1969 by Studio Vista Ltd.).

Kovel, Ralph & Terry. *Kovels' New Dictionary of Marks Pottery & Porcelain 1850 to the Present*. New York: Crown Publishers, Inc., 1986.

Little, W.L. *Staffordshire Blue*. London: B.T. Batsford, Ltd., 1969.

Mankowitz, Wolf and Reginald G. Haggar. *The Concise Encyclopedia of English Pottery and Porcelain*. New York: Hawthorne Books, Inc., n.d.

Moore, N. Hudson. *The Old China Book*. New York: Tudor Publishing Company, 1903, reprinted 1944.

Mountfield, David (comp.) *The Antique Collector's Illustrated Dictionary*. London: Hamlyn, n.d.

Snyder, Jeffrey B. *Romantic Staffordshire Ceramics*. Atglen, PA: Schiffer Publishing Ltd., 1997.

"Victorian Staffordshire Figures." *The Collector*, p. 15, June/July 1994.

Whiter, Leonard. *Spode*. New York: Praeger Publishers, 1970.

Williams, Peter. *Wedgwood, A Collector's Guide*. Radnor, PA: Wallace-Homestead, 1992.

Williams, Petra. *Flow Blue China and Mulberry Ware*. Jeffersontown, KY: Fountain House East, 1975.

___. *Staffordshire Romantic Transfer Patterns*. Jeffersontown, KY: Fountain House East, 1978.

Zeder, Audrey B. *British Royal Commemoratives*. Lombard, IL: Wallace-Homestead, 1986.

Index to Companies

(By Plate numbers)

Index to Various Types of Decorations

(By chapter or Plate number)

Index to Pattern Names

(By Plate number)

COLLECTOR BOOKS

Informing Today's Collector

For over two decades we have been keeping collectors informed on trends and values in all fields of antiques and collectibles.

DOLLS, FIGURES & TEDDY BEARS

4707	A Decade of **Barbie Dolls** & Collectibles, 1981–1991, Summers	$19.95
4631	**Barbie Doll** Boom, 1986–1995, Augustyniak	$18.95
2079	**Barbie Doll** Fashion, Volume I, Eames	$24.95
4846	**Barbie Doll** Fashion, Volume II, Eames	$24.95
3957	**Barbie** Exclusives, Rana	$18.95
4632	**Barbie** Exclusives, Book II, Rana	$18.95
5672	The **Barbie Doll** Years, 4th Ed., Olds	$19.95
3810	**Chatty Cathy** Dolls, Lewis	$15.95
5352	Collector's Ency. of **Barbie** Doll Exclusives & More, 2nd Ed.,Augustyniak	$24.95
2211	Collector's Encyclopedia of **Madame Alexander** Dolls, Smith	$24.95
4863	Collector's Encyclopedia of **Vogue Dolls**, Izen/Stover	$29.95
5821	**Doll Values**, Antique to Modern, 5th Ed., Moyer	$12.95
5829	**Madame Alexander** Collector's Dolls Price Guide #26, Crowsey	$12.95
5833	**Modern Collectible Dolls**, Volume V, Moyer	$24.95
5689	**Nippon Dolls** & Playthings, Van Patten/Lau	$29.95
5365	**Peanuts Collectibles**, Podley/Bang	$24.95
5253	Story of **Barbie**, 2nd Ed., Westenhouser	$24.95
5277	**Talking Toys** of the 20th Century, Lewis	$15.95
1513	**Teddy Bears & Steiff** Animals, Mandel	$9.95
1817	**Teddy Bears & Steiff** Animals, 2nd Series, Mandel	$19.95
2084	**Teddy Bears, Annalee's & Steiff** Animals, 3rd Series, Mandel	$19.95
5371	**Teddy Bear** Treasury, Yenke	$19.95
1808	Wonder of **Barbie**, Manos	$9.95
1430	World of **Barbie** Dolls, Manos	$9.95
4880	World of **Raggedy Ann** Collectibles, Avery	$24.95

TOYS, MARBLES & CHRISTMAS COLLECTIBLES

2333	Antique & Collectible **Marbles**, 3rd Ed., Grist	$9.95
5353	**Breyer Animal** Collector's Guide, 2nd Ed., Browell	$19.95
4976	**Christmas Ornaments**, Lights & Decorations, Johnson	$24.95
4737	**Christmas Ornaments**, Lights & Decorations, Vol. II, Johnson	$24.95
4739	**Christmas Ornaments**, Lights & Decorations, Vol. III, Johnson	$24.95
4559	Collectible **Action Figures**, 2nd Ed., Manos	$17.95
2338	Collector's Encyclopedia of **Disneyana**, Longest, Stern	$24.95
5038	Collector's Guide to **Diecast Toys** & Scale Models, 2nd Ed., Johnson	$19.95
4651	Collector's Guide to **Tinker Toys**, Strange	$18.95
4566	Collector's Guide to **Tootsietoys**, 2nd Ed., Richter	$19.95
5169	Collector's Guide to **TV Toys** & Memorabilia, 2nd Ed., Davis/Morgan	$24.95
5360	**Fisher-Price Toys**, Cassity	$19.95
4720	The Golden Age of **Automotive Toys**, 1925–1941, Hutchison/Johnson	$24.95
5593	Grist's Big Book of **Marbles**, 2nd Ed.	$24.95
3970	Grist's Machine-Made & Contemporary **Marbles**, 2nd Ed.	$9.95
5267	**Matchbox Toys**, 1947 to 1998, 3rd Ed., Johnson	$19.95
5830	**McDonald's** Collectibles, 2nd Edition, Henriques/DuVall	$24.95
5673	Modern **Candy Containers** & Novelties, Brush/Miller	$19.95
1540	Modern **Toys** 1930–1980, Baker	$19.95
3888	**Motorcycle Toys**, Antique & Contemporary, Gentry/Downs	$18.95
5693	**Schroeder's Collectible Toys**, Antique to Modern Price Guide, 7th Ed.	$17.95

FURNITURE

1457	American **Oak** Furniture, McNerney	$9.95
3716	American **Oak** Furniture, Book II, McNerney	$12.95
1118	Antique **Oak** Furniture, Hill	$7.95
2271	Collector's Encyclopedia of **American** Furniture, Vol. II, Swedberg	$24.95
3720	Collector's Encyclopedia of **American** Furniture, Vol. III, Swedberg	$24.95
5359	Early **American** Furniture, Obbard	$12.95
1755	Furniture of the **Depression Era**, Swedberg	$19.95
3906	**Heywood-Wakefield** Modern Furniture, Rouland	$18.95
1885	**Victorian** Furniture, Our American Heritage, McNerney	$9.95
3829	**Victorian** Furniture, Our American Heritage, Book II, McNerney	$9.95

JEWELRY, HATPINS, WATCHES & PURSES

1712	Antique & Collectible **Thimbles** & Accessories, Mathis	$19.95
1748	Antique **Purses**, Revised Second Ed., Holiner	$19.95
1278	Art Nouveau & Art Deco **Jewelry**, Baker	$9.95
4850	Collectible **Costume Jewelry**, Simonds	$24.95
5675	Collectible **Silver Jewelry**, Rezazadeh	$24.95
3722	Collector's Ency. of **Compacts**, Carryalls & Face Powder Boxes, Mueller	$24.95
4940	**Costume Jewelry**, A Practical Handbook & Value Guide, Rezazadeh	$24.95
1716	Fifty Years of Collectible **Fashion Jewelry**, 1925–1975, Baker	$19.95
1424	**Hatpins** & Hatpin Holders, Baker	$9.95
5695	**Ladies' Vintage Accessories**, Bruton	$24.95
1181	100 Years of Collectible **Jewelry**, 1850–1950, Baker	$9.95
4729	**Sewing Tools** & Trinkets, Thompson	$24.95
5620	Unsigned Beauties of **Costume Jewelry**, Brown	$24.95
4878	Vintage & Contemporary **Purse Accessories**, Gerson	$24.95
5696	Vintage & Vogue Ladies' **Compacts**, 2nd Edition, Gerson	$29.95

INDIANS, GUNS, KNIVES, TOOLS, PRIMITIVES

1868	Antique **Tools**, Our American Heritage, McNerney	$9.95
5616	Big Book of **Pocket Knives**, Stewart	$19.95
4943	Field Guide to Flint **Arrowheads** & Knives of the North American Indian	$9.95
2279	**Indian Artifacts** of the Midwest, Book I, Hothem	$14.95
3885	**Indian Artifacts** of the Midwest, Book II, Hothem	$16.95
4870	**Indian Artifacts** of the Midwest, Book III, Hothem	$18.95
5685	**Indian Artifacts** of the Midwest, Book IV, Hothem	$19.95
5687	**Modern Guns**, Identification & Values, 13th Ed., Quertermous	$14.95
2164	**Primitives**, Our American Heritage, McNerney	$9.95
1759	**Primitives**, Our American Heritage, 2nd Series, McNerney	$14.95
4730	Standard **Knife** Collector's Guide, 3rd Ed., Ritchie & Stewart	$12.95

PAPER COLLECTIBLES & BOOKS

4633	**Big Little Books**, Jacobs	$18.95
4710	Collector's Guide to **Children's Books**, 1850 to 1950, Volume I, Jones	$18.95
5153	Collector's Guide to **Children's Books**, 1850 to 1950, Volume II, Jones	$19.95
5596	Collector's Guide to **Children's Books**, 1950 to 1975, Volume III, Jones	$19.95
1441	Collector's Guide to **Post Cards**, Wood	$9.95
2081	Guide to Collecting **Cookbooks**, Allen	$14.95
5825	Huxford's **Old Book** Value Guide, 13th Ed.	$19.95
2080	Price Guide to **Cookbooks** & Recipe Leaflets, Dickinson	$9.95
3973	**Sheet Music** Reference & Price Guide, 2nd Ed., Pafik & Guiheen	$19.95
4654	**Victorian Trade Cards**, Historical Reference & Value Guide, Cheadle	$19.95
4733	**Whitman Juvenile Books**, Brown	$17.95

GLASSWARE

5602	Anchor Hocking's **Fire-King** & More, 2nd Ed.	$24.95
4561	Collectible **Drinking Glasses**, Chase & Kelly	$17.95
5823	Collectible **Glass Shoes**, 2nd Edition, Wheatley	$24.95
5357	Coll. **Glassware** from the 40s, 50s & 60s, 5th Ed., Florence	$19.95
1810	Collector's Encyclopedia of **American Art Glass**, Shuman	$29.95
5358	Collector's Encyclopedia of **Depression Glass**, 14th Ed., Florence	$19.95
1961	Collector's Encyclopedia of **Fry Glassware**, Fry Glass Society	$24.95
1664	Collector's Encyclopedia of **Heisey Glass**, 1925–1938, Bredehoft	$24.95
3905	Collector's Encyclopedia of **Milk Glass**, Newbound	$24.95
4936	Collector's Guide to **Candy Containers**, Dezso/Poirier	$19.95
4564	**Crackle Glass**, Weitman	$19.95
4941	**Crackle Glass**, Book II, Weitman	$19.95
4714	**Czechoslovakian Glass** and Collectibles, Book II, Barta/Rose	$16.95
5528	Early American **Pattern Glass**, Metz	$17.95
5682	**Elegant Glassware** of the Depression Era, 9th Ed., Florence	$19.95
5614	Field Guide to **Pattern Glass**, McCain	$17.95
3981	Evers' Standard **Cut Glass** Value Guide	$12.95
4659	**Fenton** Art Glass, 1907–1939, Whitmyer	$24.95
5615	Florence's **Glassware Pattern Identification** Guide, Vol. II	$19.95

COLLECTOR BOOKS
Informing Today's Collector

4719	**Fostoria**, Etched, Carved & Cut Designs, Vol. II, Kerr	$24.95
3883	**Fostoria Stemware**, The Crystal for America, Long/Seate	$24.95
5261	**Fostoria Tableware**, 1924 – 1943, Long/Seate	$24.95
5361	**Fostoria Tableware**, 1944 – 1986, Long/Seate	$24.95
5604	**Fostoria**, Useful & Ornamental, Long/Seate	$29.95
4644	**Imperial Carnival Glass**, Burns	$18.95
5827	**Kitchen Glassware** of the Depression Years, 6th Ed., Florence	$24.95
5600	Much More Early American **Pattern Glass**, Metz	$17.95
5690	Pocket Guide to **Depression Glass**, 12th Ed., Florence	$9.95
5594	Standard Encyclopedia of **Carnival Glass**, 7th Ed., Edwards/Carwile	$29.95
5595	Standard **Carnival Glass** Price Guide, 12th Ed., Edwards/Carwile	$9.95
5272	Standard Encyclopedia of **Opalescent Glass**, 3rd Ed., Edwards/Carwile	$24.95
5617	Standard Encyclopedia of **Pressed Glass**, 2nd Ed., Edwards/Carwile	$29.95
4731	**Stemware Identification**, Featuring Cordials with Values, Florence	$24.95
4732	**Very Rare Glassware** of the Depression Years, 5th Series, Florence	$24.95
4656	**Westmoreland Glass**, Wilson	$24.95

POTTERY

4927	**ABC Plates & Mugs**, Lindsay	$24.95
4929	**American Art Pottery**, Sigafoose	$24.95
4630	**American Limoges**, Limoges	$24.95
1312	**Blue & White Stoneware**, McNerney	$9.95
1958	So. Potteries **Blue Ridge Dinnerware**, 3rd Ed., Newbound	$14.95
1959	**Blue Willow**, 2nd Ed., Gaston	$14.95
4851	Collectible **Cups & Saucers**, Harran	$18.95
1373	Collector's Encyclopedia of **American Dinnerware**, Cunningham	$24.95
4931	Collector's Encyclopedia of **Bauer Pottery**, Chipman	$24.95
4932	Collector's Encyclopedia of **Blue Ridge Dinnerware**, Vol. II, Newbound	$24.95
4658	Collector's Encyclopedia of **Brush-McCoy Pottery**, Huxford	$24.95
5034	Collector's Encyclopedia of **California Pottery**, 2nd Ed., Chipman	$24.95
2133	Collector's Encyclopedia of **Cookie Jars**, Roerig	$24.95
3723	Collector's Encyclopedia of **Cookie Jars**, Book II, Roerig	$24.95
4939	Collector's Encyclopedia of **Cookie Jars**, Book III, Roerig	$24.95
5748	Collector's Encyclopedia of **Fiesta**, 9th Ed., Huxford	$24.95
4718	Collector's Encyclopedia of **Figural Planters & Vases**, Newbound	$19.95
3961	Collector's Encyclopedia of **Early Noritake**, Alden	$24.95
1439	Collector's Encyclopedia of **Flow Blue China**, Gaston	$19.95
3812	Collector's Encyclopedia of **Flow Blue China**, 2nd Ed., Gaston	$24.95
3431	Collector's Encyclopedia of **Homer Laughlin China**, Jasper	$24.95
1276	Collector's Encyclopedia of **Hull Pottery**, Roberts	$19.95
3962	Collector's Encyclopedia of **Lefton China**, DeLozier	$19.95
4855	Collector's Encyclopedia of **Lefton China**, Book II, DeLozier	$19.95
5609	Collector's Encyclopedia of **Limoges Porcelain**, 3rd Ed., Gaston	$29.95
2334	Collector's Encyclopedia of **Majolica Pottery**, Katz-Marks	$19.95
1358	Collector's Encyclopedia of **McCoy Pottery**, Huxford	$19.95
5677	Collector's Encyclopedia of **Niloak**, 2nd Edition, Gifford	$29.95
3837	Collector's Encyclopedia of **Nippon Porcelain**, Van Patten	$24.95
1665	Collector's Ency. of **Nippon Porcelain**, 3rd Series, Van Patten	$24.95
4712	Collector's Ency. of **Nippon Porcelain**, 4th Series, Van Patten	$24.95
5053	Collector's Ency. of **Nippon Porcelain**, 5th Series, Van Patten	$24.95
5678	Collector's Ency. of **Nippon Porcelain**, 6th Series, Van Patten	$29.95
1447	Collector's Encyclopedia of **Noritake**, Van Patten	$19.95
1038	Collector's Encyclopedia of **Occupied Japan**, 2nd Series, Florence	$14.95
4951	Collector's Encyclopedia of **Old Ivory China**, Hillman	$24.95
5564	Collector's Encyclopedia of **Pickard China**, Reed	$29.95
3877	Collector's Encyclopedia of **R.S. Prussia**, 4th Series, Gaston	$24.95
5679	Collector's Encyclopedia of **Red Wing Art Pottery**, Dollen	$24.95
5618	Collector's Encyclopedia of **Rosemeade Pottery**, Dommel	$24.95
5841	Collector's Encyclopedia of **Roseville Pottery**, Revised, Huxford/Nickel	$24.95
5842	Collector's Encyclopedia of **Roseville Pottery**, 2nd Series, Huxford/Nickel	$24.95
4713	Collector's Encyclopedia of **Salt Glaze Stoneware**, Taylor/Lowrance	$24.95
3314	Collector's Encyclopedia of **Van Briggle Art Pottery**, Sasicki	$24.95
4563	Collector's Encyclopedia of **Wall Pockets**, Newbound	$19.95
2111	Collector's Encyclopedia of **Weller Pottery**, Huxford	$29.95
5680	Collector's Guide to **Feather Edge Ware**, McAllister	$19.95
3876	Collector's Guide to **Lu-Ray Pastels**, Meehan	$18.95

3814	Collector's Guide to **Made in Japan Ceramics**, White	$18.95
4646	Collector's Guide to **Made in Japan Ceramics**, Book II, White	$18.95
2339	Collector's Guide to **Shawnee Pottery**, Vanderbilt	$19.95
1425	**Cookie Jars**, Westfall	$9.95
3440	**Cookie Jars**, Book II, Westfall	$19.95
4924	Figural & Novelty **Salt & Pepper Shakers**, 2nd Series, Davern	$24.95
2379	Lehner's Ency. of **U.S. Marks** on Pottery, Porcelain & China	$24.95
4722	**McCoy Pottery**, Collector's Reference & Value Guide, Hanson/Nissen	$19.95
5691	**Post86 Fiesta**, Identification & Value Guide, Racheter	$19.95
1670	**Red Wing Collectibles**, DePasquale	$9.95
1440	**Red Wing Stoneware**, DePasquale	$9.95
1632	**Salt & Pepper Shakers**, Guarnaccia	$9.95
5091	**Salt & Pepper Shakers** II, Guarnaccia	$18.95
3443	**Salt & Pepper Shakers** IV, Guarnaccia	$18.95
3738	**Shawnee Pottery**, Mangus	$24.95
4629	Turn of the Century **American Dinnerware**, 1880s–1920s, Jasper	$24.95
3327	**Watt Pottery** – Identification & Value Guide, Morris	$19.95

OTHER COLLECTIBLES

5838	Advertising **Thermometers**, Merritt	$16.95
4704	Antique & Collectible **Buttons**, Wisniewski	$19.95
2269	Antique **Brass & Copper** Collectibles, Gaston	$16.95
1880	Antique **Iron**, McNerney	$9.95
3872	Antique **Tins**, Dodge	$24.95
4845	Antique **Typewriters & Office Collectibles**, Rehr	$19.95
5607	Antiquing and Collecting on the **Internet**, Parry	$12.95
1128	**Bottle** Pricing Guide, 3rd Ed., Cleveland	$7.95
3718	Collectible **Aluminum**, Grist	$16.95
4560	Collectible **Cats**, An Identification & Value Guide, Book II, Fyke	$19.95
5060	Collectible **Souvenir Spoons**, Bednersh	$19.95
5676	Collectible **Souvenir Spoons**, Book II, Bednersh	$29.95
5666	Collector's Encyclopedia of **Granite Ware**, Book 2, Greguire	$29.95
5836	Collector's Guide to **Antique Radios**, 5th Ed., Bunis	$19.95
5608	Collector's Gde. to Buying, Selling & Trading on the **Internet**, 2nd Ed., Hix	$12.95
4637	Collector's Guide to **Cigarette Lighters**, Book II, Flanagan	$17.95
3966	Collector's Guide to **Inkwells**, Identification & Values, Badders	$18.95
4947	Collector's Guide to **Inkwells**, Book II, Badders	$19.95
5681	Collector's Guide to **Lunchboxes**, White	$19.95
5621	Collector's Guide to **Online Auctions**, Hix	$12.95
4862	Collector's Guide to **Toasters** & Accessories, Greguire	$19.95
4652	Collector's Guide to **Transistor Radios**, 2nd Ed., Bunis	$16.95
4864	Collector's Guide to **Wallace Nutting Pictures**, Ivankovich	$18.95
1629	**Doorstops**, Identification & Values, Bertoia	$9.95
5683	**Fishing Lure** Collectibles, 2nd Ed., Murphy/Edmisten	$29.95
5259	**Flea Market Trader**, 12th Ed., Huxford	$9.95
4945	**G-Men and FBI Toys** and Collectibles, Whitworth	$18.95
5605	**Garage Sale & Flea Market Annual**, 8th Ed.	$19.95
3819	**General Store** Collectibles, Wilson	$24.95
5159	**Huxford's Collectible Advertising**, 4th Ed.	$24.95
2216	**Kitchen Antiques**, 1790–1940, McNerney	$14.95
5686	**Lighting Fixtures** of the Depression Era, Book I, Thomas	$24.95
4950	The **Lone Ranger**, Collector's Reference & Value Guide, Felbinger	$18.95
2026	**Railroad** Collectibles, 4th Ed., Baker	$14.95
5619	**Roy Rogers and Dale Evans** Toys & Memorabilia, Coyle	$24.95
5692	**Schroeder's Antiques Price Guide**, 19th Ed., Huxford	$14.95
5007	**Silverplated Flatware**, Revised 4th Edition, Hagan	$18.95
5694	**Summers' Guide to Coca-Cola**, 3rd Ed.	$24.95
5356	**Summers' Pocket Guide to Coca-Cola**, 2nd Ed.	$9.95
3892	**Toy & Miniature Sewing Machines**, Thomas	$18.95
4876	**Toy & Miniature Sewing Machines**, Book II, Thomas	$24.95
5144	Value Guide to **Advertising Memorabilia**, 2nd Ed., Summers	$19.95
3977	Value Guide to **Gas Station Memorabilia**, Summers & Priddy	$24.95
4877	Vintage **Bar Ware**, Visakay	$24.95
4935	The W.F. Cody **Buffalo Bill** Collector's Guide with Values	$24.95
5281	**Wanted to Buy**, 7th Edition	$9.95